AMERICA'S STORY

BOOK ONE
TO 1865

By VIVIAN BERNSTEIN

Reviewers

John Alexander
Social Studies Consultant
Jefferson Parish Schools
Harvey, LA

Dr. John L. Esposito
Georgetown University
Washington, D.C.

Eric R. Godoy
Teacher of Second Language Learners
West Chicago Elementary School District
West Chicago, IL

Harcourt Achieve

Rigby • Saxon • Steck-Vaughn

www.HarcourtAchieve.com
1.800.531.5015

About the Author

Vivian Bernstein is the author of *America's History: Land of Liberty, World History and You, World Geography and You, American Government, and Decisions for Health.* She received her Master of Arts degree from New York University. Bernstein is active with professional organizations in social studies, education, and reading. She gives presentations to school faculties and professional groups about social studies instruction and improving content area reading. Bernstein was a teacher in the New York City Public School System for a number of years.

Staff Credits

Executive Editor: Tina Posner
Supervising Editor: Donna Townsend
Editor: Linda Doehne

Design Staff: Stephanie Arsenault, Donna Cunningham, Joan Cunignham, Deborah Diver, John-Paxton Gremillion, Scott Huber, Heather Jernt, Alan Klemp, Joyce Spicer

Acknowledgments

Cartography: MapQuest.com, Inc., Ortelius Design, Inc.

Photo Credits: Cover: (bkgd) Donnovan Reese/Getty Images; (a) ©The Granger Collection, New York; (c) ©Corbis; (d) ©Dennis Macdonald/PhotoEdit; (e) ©Corbis

Additional Photography by Comstock Royalty Free and Getty Images Royalty Free.
i ©Donovan Reese/Getty Images; x (a) ©Associated Press, AP; (b) ©Stone/Getty Images; xi (a) ©Jeff Greenbert/Index Stock Imagery; (b) ©SuperStock/PictureQuest; (c) ©Brand X Pictures/PicturQuest; 4–6, 9 ©The Granger Collection; 10 (a, b) ©The Granger Collection (c) ©North Wind Picture Archives;14 ©The Granger Collection; 15 (a) ©Bettmann/Corbis; (b) ©North Wind Picture Archives; 16 ©North Wind Picture Archives; 17 ©Eric Neurath/Stock Boston; 20–22 ©The Granger Collection; 23 ©North Wind Picture Archives; 24 ©Photodisc/Getty Royalty Free/HA Collection; 25–26 ©The Granger Collection; 27 (a, b) ©The Granger Collection; (c) ©Bettmann/Corbis; 28 ©Courtesy of APVA Preservation Virginia; 31 ©The Granger Collection; 32 (a) ©Bettmann/Corbis; (b, c) ©The Granger Collection; 33 ©The Granger Collection; 34 ©North Wind Picture Archives; 38–41 (a) ©The Granger Collection; (b) ©North Wind Picture Archives; 42 ©The Granger Collection; 43 ©Bettmann/Corbis; 46 ©Bettmann/Corbis; 47 (a) ©The Granger Collection; (b) ©Reagan Bradshaw/HA Collection; (c) ©The Granger Collection; 48 (a) ©The Valentine Richmond History Center; (b, c) ©The Granger Collection; 49 (a) ©The Granger Collection; (b) ©Bettmann/Corbis; 50 ©Faustinus Dareat/HA Collection; 53 ©Bettmann/Corbis; 54 ©The Granger Collection; 55 (a, b) ©The Granger Collection; 58 ©Archivo Iconografico, S.A./Corbis; 59 (a) ©The Granger Collection; (b) Walter Bibikow/Taxi/Getty Images; 60–61 (a) ©The Granger Collection; (b) ©North Wind Picture Archives; 62 Stone/Getty images; 65 ©The Granger Collection; 66 (a) ©Reagan Bradshaw/HA Collection; (b) Pan America/Picturequest; 67 (a) ©Reagan Bradshaw/HA Collection; (b) ©Photos.com; (c) ©Pan America/Picturequest; 68 (a) AFP/Getty Images; (b) ©Bob Daemmrich; 72–74 ©The Granger Collection; 75 (a) ©Bettmann/Corbis; (b) ©North Wind Picture Archives; (c) ©The Granger Collection; 76 ©courtesy Missouri Historical Society, St. Louis; 77, 80–81 (a, b) ©The Granger Collection; (c) ©Stock Montage; 82 (b) ©North Wind Picture Archives; (c) ©The Granger Collection; 83, 87 ©The Granger Collection; 88 (a) ©Hulton Archive/Getty Images; (b) ©North Wind Picture Archives; (c) ©Kevin Fleming /Corbis; 89 ©The Granger Collection; 90, 93–94 ©The Granger Collection; 95 ©The New York Public Library/Art Resource, NY; 96 ©North Wind Picture Archives; 97, 101 ©The Granger Collection; 102 (a) ©Brown Brothers; (b) ©Mount Holyoke College Art Museum, South Hadley, MA; (c) ©The Granger Collection; 103 (a) ©Corbis; (b) ©Bettmann/Corbis; 104 (a) ©Bettmann/Corbis; (b) ©The Granger Collection; 108–109 ©courtesy The Bucks County Historical Society, Doylestown, PA; 110 ©North Wind Picture Archives; 111(a) ©North Wind Picture Archives; (b, c) ©Courtesy University of Texas; 112 (a) ©courtesy The Institute for Texan Cultures; (b) ©courtesy The Barker Texas History Center, University of Texas, Austin; (c) ©courtesy The Institute for Texan Cultures; (d) ©The Granger Collection; 113 (a) ©courtesy of the State Preservation Board, Austin, Texas. CHA 1989.46, Photographer Unknown, pre 1991, pre conservation; (b) ©courtesy The Institute for Texan Cultures; (c) ©Quinn Stewart; 116 Texas State Library and Archive Commission; 117 (a) ©The Bettmann Archive/Corbis; (b) ©The Granger Collection; 119, 122 ©North Wind Picture Archives; 124–125 ©The Granger Collection;126 ©Brown Brothers; 130–132 ©The Granger Collection; 133 (a) ©The Bettmann Archive/Corbis; (b) ©The Granger Collection; (c) ©Corbis; 134, 138 ©The Granger Collection; 139 (a) ©Quinn Stewart; (b) ©The Granger Collection

ISBN 0-7398-9710-1

Contents

To the Reader

America's Story tells the story of our country. Our country is the United States of America. This book tells how the United States began. It also tells how the United States changed from a small country to a large country.

Our country's story began with Native Americans. Later, people came to America from Europe. Great Britain ruled 13 colonies in America. Time passed, and Americans in the 13 colonies fought and won a war against the British. After the war, the colonies became a free country. This country was called the United States of America. The leaders of the United States wrote new laws. The laws protected the freedom of the people.

At first, the United States had only 13 states. Slowly, more and more states became part of the United States.

As the country grew, problems between the northern and southern states also grew. People in the North and South did not agree about slavery. Some southern states decided to leave the United States. They started a new nation. This led to a long, hard war. After the war, the United States became one nation again.

While you read *America's Story*, you can become a better student if you follow these steps. Start by learning the New Words for each chapter. Study the maps and pictures in each chapter. Then read the chapter carefully. Finally, think carefully as you write your answers for the "Using What You've Learned" pages.

As you read this book, you will learn how different Americans built this country. Read on and learn how people have worked to make our country a land of freedom for more than 225 years.

Vivian Bernstein

The Five Themes of Geography

Geography is the study of Earth and the people, plants, and animals that live on it. Geographers divide geography into five **themes**, or main ideas. When you know the five themes, you can begin to think like a geographer.

Movement

How do people, ideas, and goods move? People travel on the Acela train at speeds of up to 150 miles an hour.

Place

What makes a place special? The city of San Francisco is built on steep hills.

Location

Where is a place located? Pittsburgh, Pennsylvania, is found where the Allegheny River and the Monongahela River join to form the Ohio River.

Human-Environment Interaction

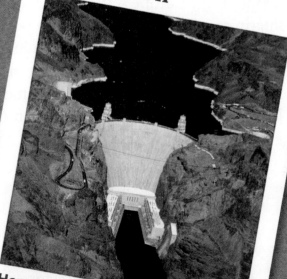

How do people change the place they live? People built the Hoover Dam to control the Colorado River. Now the river stores water for cities and farms and makes electric power.

Region

How is one area different from another? The Midwest is a part of the United States where fields of corn and wheat stretch for miles.

The Settlers of America

What do you think it was like to go across an ocean hundreds of years ago? You would not see land for many days. No one would come to help you if you lost your way. You might get sick. Rats might eat the food on your ship. Yet hundreds of years ago, brave people took this dangerous trip to come to America.

About 500 years ago, people from Europe started coming to America. People came for different reasons. Some came to explore. Others came to find gold. Still others came because they wanted more freedom. Many people from Europe settled in America. The Pilgrims were one group. But the people from Europe were not the first to live here. Native Americans had been living in America for thousands of years. American Indians helped the Pilgrims and some other groups of settlers live in America.

Read to Learn

- How did Native Americans live their lives?
- Who were the people from Europe who explored and settled in America?
- Why did different groups of people make the dangerous trip to America?

Christopher Columbus reaches America.
1492

1400   1500

Cartier explores the St. Lawrence River for France. **1534**

The English start Jamestown, Virginia. **1607**

The last English colony is started in Georgia. **1733**

England wins the French and Indian War. **1763**

1600

1700

1800

1540 Coronado explores the Southwest for Spain.

1619 Captured Africans are brought to Jamestown.

1682 LaSalle explores the Mississippi River for France.

1754 The French and Indian War begins.

3

NEW WORDS

religions
cotton
buffalo

PEOPLE & PLACES

American Indians
America
Asia
Alaska
Native Americans
United States
 of America
Americans
Northwest
Southwest
Midwest
Great Plains
East

The First Americans

➔ **Learning from Pictures How did Native Americans of the Northwest get food?**

Native Americans were the first people to live in America. Long ago they lived in Asia. It is believed that land once connected Asia and America. People moved across this land to a part of America called Alaska. Over time they settled in many parts of America. Native Americans are sometimes called American Indians.

Thousands of years later, people from other lands began coming to America. About 230 years ago, the name of our country became the United States of America. Native Americans lived in our country long before it was called the United States. Native Americans were the first Americans.

Native Americans in different parts of the United States spoke different languages. They also lived in different kinds of houses. They wore different kinds of clothes. They ate different kinds of foods. They believed in different **religions**.

Long ago people walked across land from Asia into America.

Areas of the United States where different groups of Native Americans lived

Native Americans who lived on the Great Plains hunted buffalo.

Many Native Americans lived in the Northwest of the United States. In the Northwest, there were thick forests. There were many fish in the ocean and rivers. Native Americans of the Northwest went fishing to get food. They ate fish every day. They traveled in long canoes made from trees in the forest. They also built houses from trees.

Other groups of Native Americans lived in the Southwest. In the Southwest, there was little rain. There were few trees. There were very few fish and animals to eat. Native Americans of the Southwest became farmers. They used river water to grow food. They grew corn and beans for food. They also grew **cotton**. They made their clothes from cotton.

In the Midwest of the United States, the land is very flat. We call this flat land the Great Plains. Millions of **buffalo** lived on the Great Plains. Many Native Americans lived on the Great Plains. They became buffalo hunters. They used every part of the buffalo that they killed. They ate buffalo meat. They made needles from buffalo bones. They made clothes and tents out of buffalo skins.

In the East of the United States, there were many forests. Animals lived in the forests. Many groups of Native Americans lived in these forests. They became hunters. They killed deer and turkeys for food. They also became farmers. They grew corn, pumpkins, and beans for their families.

▲ **Native Americans who lived on the Great Plains made tents out of buffalo skins.**

There were some ways that all Native Americans were alike. They loved plants and animals. They took good care of their land. They enjoyed games and telling stories.

All Native Americans made their own tools. They needed tools for hunting, farming, and fishing. Native Americans made their tools out of stones and animal bones. They made knives out of stones. Some groups of Native Americans made metal tools. Many Native Americans hunted with bows and arrows. They did not have guns.

When people later came to America, Native Americans taught them many things. They taught them how to plant foods such as corn, tomatoes, and potatoes. They also taught people how to use plants to make medicines.

There are many Native Americans in the United States today. They enjoy old and modern ways of life. Many now work at different kinds of jobs. They also still enjoy songs, dances, games, and stories that people enjoyed long ago. Many people like to buy beautiful Native American art. Native Americans today are proud that they were the first people to build our country. They are proud that they were the first Americans.

Using What You've Learned

Read and Remember

Choose a Word Choose a word in blue print to finish each sentence. Write the word on the correct blank.

> Americans fishing medicines
> corn   buffalo hunters

1. Native Americans were the first _____ .

2. Native Americans who lived in the Northwest went _____ for their food.

3. Native American farmers of the Southwest grew beans and _____ .

4. Animals that lived on the Great Plains were the _____ .

5. Native Americans who lived on the Great Plains became _____ .

6. Native Americans used special plants to make _____ .

Think and Apply

Fact or Opinion A **fact** is a true statement. An **opinion** is a statement that tells what a person thinks.

> **Fact** The land is very flat in the Midwest.

> **Opinion** The Midwest is the best place to live.

Write F next to each fact below. Write O next to each opinion. You should find two sentences that are opinions.

_____ 1. Native Americans spoke different languages.

_____ 2. Millions of buffalo lived on the Great Plains.

_____ 3. It was easy to live on the Great Plains.

_____ 4. Native Americans made tools from stones and bones.

_____ 5. The best tools were made from stones.

Skill Builder

Understanding Continents We live on the planet Earth. Earth has large bodies of land called **continents**. There are seven continents. Most continents have many countries. We live on the continent of North America. Our country, the United States, is in North America.

Here is a list of the continents in order of their size. The largest continent is first on the list.

1. Asia
2. Africa
3. North America
4. South America
5. Antarctica
6. Europe
7. Australia

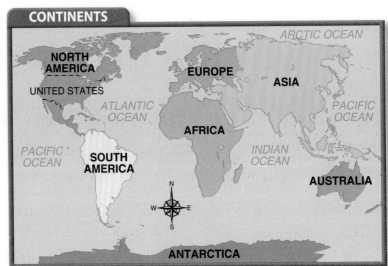

Look at the map above. Write a sentence to answer each question.

1. What are the seven continents? _____

   _____

2. Which continent has the United States? _____

   _____

3. Which is the largest continent?_____

4. Which ocean separates North America from Africa and Europe? _____

   _____

Journal Writing

Think about the different groups of Native Americans. Choose two groups. Write about where they lived. Then tell how they got food. Write four to six sentences in your journal.

Christopher Columbus

Find Out

❶ Which people knew about America before Columbus took his trip?

❷ Where did Columbus want to go?

❸ Why did Queen Isabella help Columbus?

NEW WORDS

spices
claimed
New World

PEOPLE & PLACES

Christopher
  Columbus
Italy
Atlantic Ocean
Europe
India
China
Queen Isabella
Spain
Bahamas

Learning from Pictures How did these explorers feel when they reached land?

Christopher Columbus lived long ago. Columbus was born around 1451 in Italy. He became a sailor. He also made maps.

In the 1400s, people knew less about the world than we know today. No one knew how large the Atlantic Ocean really was. Some people believed the world was flat. No one in Europe knew there was the land we now call America. Only Native Americans knew about their land.

At that time, people from Europe went to India and China to get jewels, silks, and **spices**. India and China are on the continent of Asia. People traveled thousands of miles to the east to reach India and China. Their route was long and dangerous.

Christopher Columbus wanted to find an easier way to travel to Asia. Columbus thought the world was round. He believed he could go to India by sailing west across the Atlantic Ocean.

Columbus needed ships and sailors to sail across the Atlantic Ocean. Columbus went to see Isabella, the queen of Spain. Queen Isabella thought about Columbus's plan for seven years. She thought that Columbus might reach India by sailing across the Atlantic Ocean. She wanted Columbus to find gold for Spain. So Queen Isabella decided to help him.

Queen Isabella gave Columbus three small ships. The names of the ships were the *Niña*, the *Pinta*, and the *Santa María*.

Columbus wanted to become rich from his trip. He wanted gold. Queen Isabella said Columbus could keep some of the gold he might find.

Columbus and the sailors sailed west across the Atlantic Ocean for more than a month. They did not see

Queen Isabella gave Christopher Columbus three ships.

Columbus sailed with three ships—the *Niña*, the *Pinta*, and the *Santa María*. ▶

"The crew of the *Niña* saw other signs of land, and a stalk loaded with rose berries. These signs encouraged them, and they all grew cheerful."

–from The Log of Christopher Columbus

land for many days. The sailors were afraid. They wanted to turn back for Spain. But Columbus was brave. He said to sail until October 12. Then they would turn back if they did not see land.

On October 12, 1492, the sailors saw land. On that day the three ships reached a small island.

Columbus thought he was in India. But he was not in India. He was on a small island in the Americas. The island was part of a group of islands. Today these islands are a country called the Bahamas.

People already lived on the island where Christopher Columbus landed. Columbus called these people Indians because he thought he was in India. Now they are known as Native Americans.

Columbus **claimed** America for Spain. For the people of Europe, America was a **New World**. Of course, it was not a new world to the Native Americans who lived there. Soon after Columbus's trip, more people from Europe began to come to America.

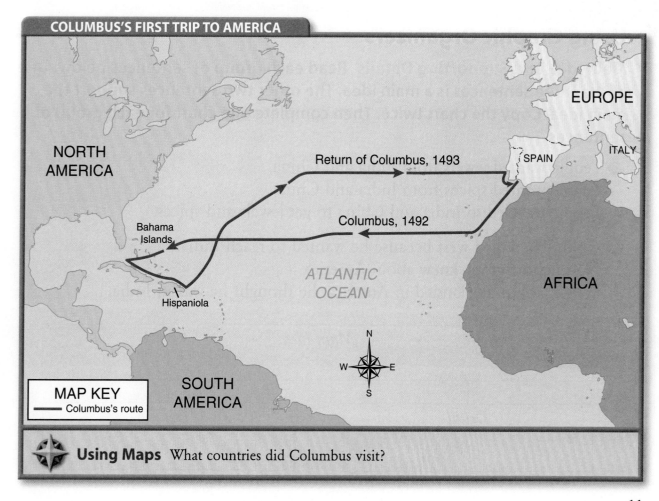

COLUMBUS'S FIRST TRIP TO AMERICA

EUROPE

NORTH AMERICA

SPAIN

ITALY

Return of Columbus, 1493

Columbus, 1492

Bahama Islands

ATLANTIC OCEAN

AFRICA

Hispaniola

N
W   E
S

MAP KEY
— Columbus's route

SOUTH AMERICA

Using Maps What countries did Columbus visit?

11

Using What You've Learned

Read and Remember

Choose the Answer Draw a circle around the correct answer.

1. Why did people from Europe want to go to India and China?
   to travel   to get jewels, silks, and spices   to see buffalo

2. Where did Columbus want to go?
   America   India   Europe

3. What did Queen Isabella give to Columbus?
   jewels   ships   spices

4. What ocean did Columbus sail across?
   Pacific Ocean   Indian Ocean   Atlantic Ocean

5. When did Columbus reach America?
   1412   1451   1492

Using Graphic Organizers

Main Idea and Supporting Details Read each group of sentences below. One of the three sentences is a main idea. The other two sentences support the main idea. Copy the chart twice. Then complete one chart for each group of sentences.

1. People wanted jewels from India and China.
   People wanted spices from India and China.
   People traveled to India and China to get jewels and spices.

2. Columbus sailed west because he wanted to reach India.
   No one in Europe knew about America.
   When Columbus landed in America, he thought he was in India.

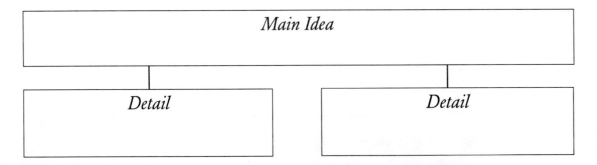

12

Skill Builder

Using Map Directions The four main directions are **north**, **south**, **east**, and **west**. On maps, these directions are shown by a **compass rose**. You can also use the letters, **N**, **S**, **E**, and **W** to show directions on a compass rose.

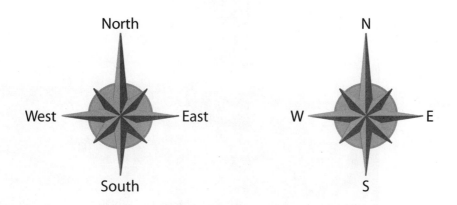

Look back at the map on page 11. Then finish each sentence with the word north, south, east, or west.

1. Europe is _____ of the Atlantic Ocean.

2. North America is _____ of the Atlantic Ocean.

3. South America is _____ of North America.

4. Europe is _____ of Africa.

5. Africa is _____ of South America and North America.

6. The Bahama Islands are _____ of Africa.

The Spanish Explore America

Learning from Pictures **How can you tell that this explorer is in a desert?**

Christopher Columbus claimed America for Spain in 1492. Soon people from Spain began to travel across the Atlantic Ocean. They settled in Mexico and South America.

The Spanish heard stories about seven cities that were made of gold. The Spanish wanted to find the cities. They began to explore the land north of Mexico. Today this area is part of the Southwest of the United States.

One of the first people to explore the Southwest for Spain was Estevanico. He was an African. In 1539 Estevanico searched the Southwest for the seven cities of gold. He never found gold. Some think he was killed by Native Americans.

Francisco Coronado

Hernando de Soto

Francisco Coronado also wanted to find the cities of gold. In 1540 he and 300 Spanish soldiers went to the Southwest. Coronado searched for two years. He found Native American farmers and villages in the Southwest. But he never found the seven cities of gold. In 1542 Coronado went home to Mexico. The king of Spain said the Southwest belonged to Spain.

Hernando de Soto also wanted to find the seven cities of gold for Spain. De Soto started in Florida with more than 700 people in 1539. While he was looking for gold, he came to a very wide river. It was the Mississippi River. He was the first person from Europe to see this river. De Soto never found the seven cities of gold. The Spanish king said that the Southeast area De Soto explored belonged to Spain, too.

Native Americans and the Spanish learned from one another. Native Americans taught the Spanish to grow beans, tomatoes, corn, pumpkins, and cotton. The Spanish brought animals from Europe. They brought

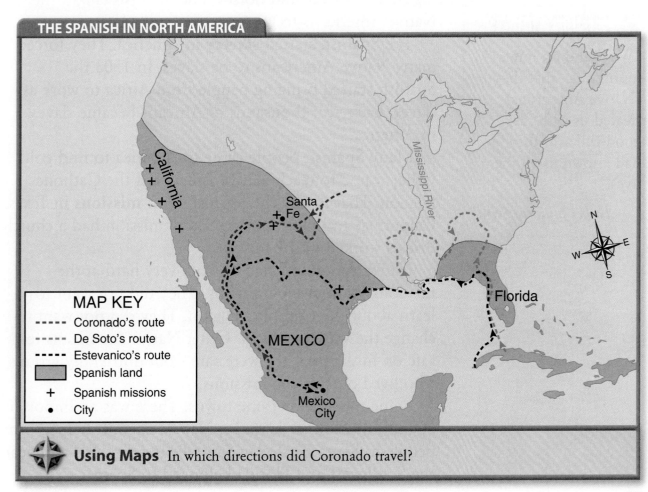

THE SPANISH IN NORTH AMERICA

California

Santa Fe

Mississippi River

Florida

MEXICO

Mexico City

MAP KEY
- - - - Coronado's route
- - - - De Soto's route
- - - - Estevanico's route
Spanish land
+ Spanish missions
• City

Using Maps In which directions did Coronado travel?

The Spanish built many missions in North America to teach Native Americans the Catholic religion. ➤

pigs, cows, sheep, and horses. The Spanish taught the Native Americans to grow oranges and wheat.

The Spanish started **slavery** in America. They forced many Native Americans to be slaves. In 1503 the Spanish started bringing people from Africa to work as slaves. Each year thousands of Africans became slaves in America.

Many Spanish people came to America to find gold. Others came to teach Native Americans the Catholic religion. That is why the Spanish built **missions** in Texas, California, and New Mexico. Every mission had a church. **Priests** worked in the missions.

Native Americans had to work very hard at the missions. Many were unhappy. They did not want to learn about the Catholic religion. They did not want to change the way they lived. Other Native Americans felt safe on missions. They were safe from unfriendly groups who lived outside the missions.

Some missions became towns. There was an important Spanish mission in Santa Fe, New Mexico. It helped bring people to Santa Fe. Today Santa Fe is a city. For 300 years the Southwest and Florida belonged to Spain.

Using Geography Themes

Place: Santa Fe, New Mexico

Geographers use five **themes**, or main ideas, to learn about different areas and people on Earth. The theme of **place** tells what makes an area different from other areas in the world. Place tells about an area's land, plants, and weather. It also tells about an area's people and what they built there.

Read the paragraphs about Santa Fe. Study the photo and the map.

Santa Fe is the **capital** of New Mexico. It is in the Southwest of the United States. The Spanish built it around 1610. Santa Fe is in high hills near the Sangre de Cristo Mountains. It is the highest and oldest capital in the nation. It has many buildings made from bricks of dried mud.

Many Pueblo Indians live in villages around Santa Fe. Pueblo Indians lived in the Santa Fe area long before the Spanish came. In 1610 the Spanish built a mission in Santa Fe for Native Americans. Today it is called the San Miguel Mission.

On your paper, write the answer to each question.

1. In what area of the United States is Santa Fe, New Mexico?
2. What mountains are near Santa Fe?
3. What are many buildings in Santa Fe made of?
4. Who live in the villages around Santa Fe?
5. Look at the map. What river goes through Santa Fe?
6. What are two buildings that people built in Santa Fe?

Using What You've Learned

Read and Remember

Finish the Sentence Draw a circle around the word or words that finish each sentence.

1 One of the first people to explore the Southwest for Spain was _____ .
Estevanico   Columbus   De Soto

2 Coronado explored the _____ of the United States.
Northwest   Southwest   Southeast

3 De Soto looked for gold in _____ .
Florida   New Mexico   California

4 De Soto was the first person from Europe to see the _____ .
Atlantic Ocean   Northeast   Mississippi River

5 Estevanico, Coronado, and De Soto tried to find the _____ cities of gold.
five   six   seven

6 The Spanish built _____ for the Native Americans.
farms   stores   missions

Think and Apply

Categories Read the words in each group. Decide how they are alike. Choose the best title in blue print for each group. Write the title on the line above each group. The first one is done for you.

Hernando de Soto   **King of Spain**
Francisco Coronado   **Explorers**

1 <u>Francisco Coronado</u>
looked for seven cities of gold
explored the Southwest
found Native American villages

2 _____
said the Southwest belonged to Spain
said the Southeast belonged to Spain
ruler of Spain

3 _____

Estevanico
Francisco Coronado
Hernando de Soto

4 _____

looked for seven cities of gold
explored Florida
saw the Mississippi River

Skill Builder _____

Using a Map Key Maps often show many things. Sometimes a map uses little drawings to show what something on the map means. A **map key** tells what those drawings mean. Look at the map key below. On the correct blanks, write what each drawing means.

```
MAP KEY
- - - - -  Coronado's route
- - - - -  De Soto's route
- - - - -  Estevanico's route
[____]     Spanish land
  +        Spanish missions
  •        City
```

+ **1** _____

• **2** _____

[____] **3** _____

- - - - - **4** _____

Use the map and map key on page 15 to finish these sentences. Circle the number or word that finishes each sentence.

1 There are _____ missions on this map.
20   10   7

2 There were _____ missions in California.
4   10   15

3 The _____ River is on the map.
Mississippi   Florida   Santa Fe

4 De Soto's route began in the _____ .
east   north   west

5 Coronado's route began in the _____ .
north   south   east

19

The Pilgrims' Thanksgiving

NEW WORDS

Church of England
freedom of religion
Mayflower Compact
governor
colony
peace treaty

PEOPLE & PLACES

Pilgrims
England
Holland
Dutch
English
Massachusetts
Plymouth
Wampanoag
Massasoit
Squanto

Learning from Pictures Why did the Pilgrims bring their families with them?

A long time ago, the Pilgrims lived in England. All the people in England had to pray in the king's church. This church was called the **Church of England**. The Pilgrims did not like the Church of England. They wanted to pray in their own church.

The Pilgrims left England and went to a small country called Holland. There was **freedom of religion** in Holland. The Pilgrims prayed in their own church in Holland.

The people of Holland are called the Dutch. They speak the Dutch language. The Pilgrims did not like living in Holland. They wanted to keep their English ways. They decided to go to America. In America they could live as they wanted and have freedom of religion.

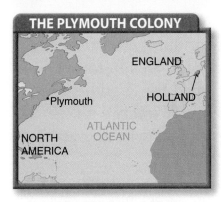

THE PLYMOUTH COLONY

ENGLAND

Plymouth

HOLLAND

ATLANTIC
OCEAN

NORTH
AMERICA

The Pilgrims traveled across the Atlantic Ocean.

The *Mayflower*

> **Learning from Pictures What did Squanto use to help make corn grow?** ➤

In 1620 the Pilgrims left Holland for America. They had a ship. Their ship was the *Mayflower*. The trip took 66 days. The weather was rainy and cold. Many Pilgrims became sick during the long, cold trip.

At last the *Mayflower* reached America. It landed in Massachusetts. Before leaving their ship, the Pilgrims made a plan for a government. That plan was the **Mayflower Compact**. The plan said the Pilgrims would work together to make laws. The laws would be fair to all. The Pilgrims would not have a king in America. They would choose a **governor** and rule themselves. The Mayflower Compact was the first government in America that allowed people from Europe to rule themselves.

The Pilgrims landed in November. They started a **colony** called Plymouth. Plymouth was the second English colony in America. In Chapter 5, you will read about the first English colony in America.

The first winter in Plymouth was very cold. There was little food. Many Pilgrims became sick and died.

There were no groups of Native Americans in Plymouth when the Pilgrims landed. But the Wampanoag were a group of Native Americans who lived in forests near Plymouth. They came and helped the Pilgrims. Their leader was Massasoit. He signed a **peace treaty** with the Pilgrims. The Pilgrims and the Wampanoag lived together in peace.

Squanto was a Native American who taught the Pilgrims how to plant corn. He showed the Pilgrims where to find many fish. He taught the Pilgrims to hunt for deer and turkeys in the forests.

The Pilgrims worked hard in Plymouth. They planted seeds to grow food. They built a church. They built houses. By November 1621 the Pilgrims had a lot of food.

The Pilgrims had a Thanksgiving party in November 1621. They invited their Wampanoag friends. The Wampanoag brought deer. The Pilgrims brought turkeys. This Thanksgiving lasted three days. The Pilgrims gave thanks to God for helping them. They said "thank you" to the Wampanoag for helping them. This was the Pilgrims' first Thanksgiving in America.

▲ **The Pilgrims and the Wampanoag enjoyed a Thanksgiving party in 1621.**

Using What You've Learned

Read and Remember

Choose the Answer Draw a circle around the correct answer.

1. Where did the Pilgrims first live?
   Holland   England   America

2. Why did the Pilgrims come to America?
   to farm   to have freedom of religion   to meet Native Americans

3. What was the name of the Pilgrims' ship?
   Niña   Mayflower   Pinta

4. What town in America did the Pilgrims start?
   Massachusetts   Plymouth   Santa Fe

Think and Apply

Cause and Effect A **cause** is something that makes something else happen. What happens is called the **effect**.

Cause   The Pilgrims wanted fair laws

Effect   so they wrote the Mayflower Compact.

Match each cause on the left with an effect on the right. Write the letter of the effect on the correct blank. The first one is done for you.

Cause

1. The Pilgrims did not want to pray in the Church of England, so __d__

2. The Pilgrims could not keep their English ways in Holland, so _____

3. The Pilgrims had little food for their first winter, so _____

4. The Wampanoag wanted peace so, _____

5. The Pilgrims had a lot of food for their second winter, so _____

Effect

a. many Pilgrims died.

b. Massasoit signed a peace treaty with the Pilgrims.

c. they had a Thanksgiving party to thank God and the Wampanoag.

d. they went to Holland.

e. they went to America.

23

Skill Builder

Reading a Flow Chart A **flow chart** is a chart that shows you facts in their correct order. The flow chart on this page shows how the Wampanoag grew corn in fields in the 1600s. Whole kernels are the seeds of the corn plant. A hoe is a tool for digging in soil.

Read the flow chart. Then circle the word or words that finish each sentence below.

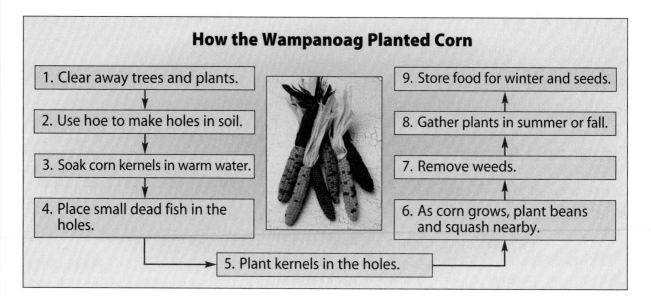

How the Wampanoag Planted Corn

1. Clear away trees and plants.
2. Use hoe to make holes in soil.
3. Soak corn kernels in warm water.
4. Place small dead fish in the holes.
5. Plant kernels in the holes.
6. As corn grows, plant beans and squash nearby.
7. Remove weeds.
8. Gather plants in summer or fall.
9. Store food for winter and seeds.

1. The first step is to _____ trees.
   shake   clear away   plant

2. The Wampanoag placed _____ with the kernels in the holes.
   fish   worms   weeds

3. In Step 6 beans and _____ are planted nearby.
   squash   tomatoes   orange trees

4. The last step is to _____ some food.
   store   grow   burn

Journal Writing

Write a paragraph in your journal that tells why the Pilgrims gave thanks. Give at least three reasons why they might have been thankful.

The English Settle America

➤ **Learning from Pictures** **What did the English do to start a colony in Jamestown?**

The Pilgrims were not the first group of English people to live in America. The first group of English people came to America in 1585, but their colony failed.

Before long more English people moved to America. They came for three reasons. Many people came to get rich. Some people came for freedom of religion. Others came because they thought they could have a better life.

In 1607 the English started another colony in America. It was called Jamestown. It was in Virginia. At first the Jamestown **settlers** did not want to grow food or build houses. They did not want to plant seed to grow food. They only wanted to look for gold. The settlers were very hungry during the first winter. Many settlers died. More people came to live in Jamestown. Then the settlers began to work harder. They built farms and houses.

In 1619 the Jamestown settlers made Africans help them grow tobacco.

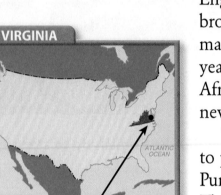

Jamestown

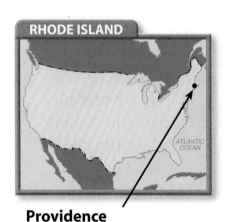

Providence

The settlers began to grow **tobacco**. People smoked tobacco in pipes. The settlers sold their tobacco to England for a lot of money. In 1619 Dutch traders brought captured Africans to Jamestown. The settlers made the Africans help them grow tobacco. After some years, the Africans were freed. Later large numbers of Africans were forced to work as slaves. They were never freed.

The Puritans were a group of people who did not want to pray in the Church of England. In 1628 a group of Puritans came to Massachusetts for freedom of religion. The Puritans started the first schools in America. Everyone in Massachusetts had to pray in Puritan churches. The Puritans did not let other people have freedom of religion.

Roger Williams lived with the Puritans. He told them that everyone should have freedom of religion. He left Massachusetts and traveled through the forests. Roger Williams met Native Americans who helped him. He bought land from them. Roger Williams started the city of Providence on that land in 1636. Later, the land became the colony of Rhode Island. Providence was the first city in America where there was freedom of religion for all.

Anne Hutchinson was a woman who lived in Massachusetts. Her **religious** ideas were different from the Puritan ideas. Hutchinson also left Massachusetts. She went to Rhode Island in 1638 and started a new town.

William Penn brought settlers to Pennsylvania.

James Oglethorpe helped people move to Georgia.

Anne Hutchinson's ideas were different from the ideas of other Puritans. ➤

More English people came to America for freedom of religion. Catholics were sent to jail if they prayed in Catholic churches in England. So 92 Catholics came to America in 1634. They started a colony called Maryland.

People from Holland had started a colony near the Atlantic Ocean in 1624. Then in 1664 England took control of the Dutch colony. It became an English colony. It was called New York.

The Quakers were another group of people who would not pray in the Church of England. William Penn was a Quaker. In 1681 the English king gave Penn some land in America. Penn started the Pennsylvania colony on that land. Penn also bought the land from Native Americans who lived there. The Native Americans liked Penn. People had freedom of religion in Pennsylvania.

In England there were some people who did not have any money. People who were **in debt** were put into jail. These people could not work or help their families. James Oglethorpe started the Georgia colony to help these people. In 1733 Oglethorpe went to Georgia with 120 of these people. Poor people from many countries in Europe also moved to the Georgia colony.

Each year more people came to live in the English colonies. By 1753 there were 13 English colonies along the Atlantic Ocean.

Using Primary Sources

Objects from Jamestown

Primary sources are the words and objects of people who have lived at different times. Some primary sources are journals, newspapers, and tools. These words and objects help us learn about people's lives and about history.

We know what life was like in Jamestown from objects that were found there. Parts of beds, curtains, and cooking pots teach us how the settlers lived. Helmets give us clues about how the settlers protected themselves. People have found knives for cutting in Jamestown. They also have found tools for building houses.

The objects on this page were found in the earth at Jamestown. They are from the 1600s. These objects help us understand how Jamestown settlers lived almost 400 years ago.

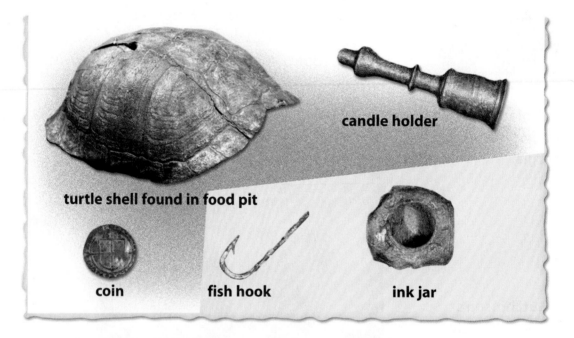

candle holder

turtle shell found in food pit

coin

fish hook

ink jar

On your paper, write the answer to each question.

1. How do we know the Jamestown settlers used money?
2. What object shows that some settlers could read and write?
3. What do you think the settlers did with candles?
4. What are two foods that the settlers probably ate?
5. **Think and Write** How do the objects from Jamestown compare with similar objects today? How have they changed?

Using What You've Learned

Read and Remember

Write the Answer Write a sentence to answer each question.

1. What were three reasons English people came to America? _____
   _____

2. What did captured Africans do in Jamestown? _____
   _____

3. Why did the Puritans come to America? _____
   _____

Using Graphic Organizers

Sequencing Events Read each of the sentences below. Copy and then complete the graphic organizer by listing the events in the correct order.

The English started Jamestown, one of the first colonies in America.

Roger Williams and Anne Hutchinson left Massachusetts to have freedom of religion.

In 1681 William Penn started the peaceful colony of Pennsylvania.

The Puritans started a colony in Massachusetts in 1628.

1.
2.
3.
4.

Journal Writing

Which colony would you want to live in if you had moved to America in 1755? Write a paragraph in your journal that tells which colony you would choose. Explain your reasons.

Skill Builder

Reading a Historical Map A **historical map** shows how an area used to look. The historical map on this page shows the 13 English colonies in the year 1753. The 13 colonies are numbered on the map in the order that people from Europe first settled there. Study the map.

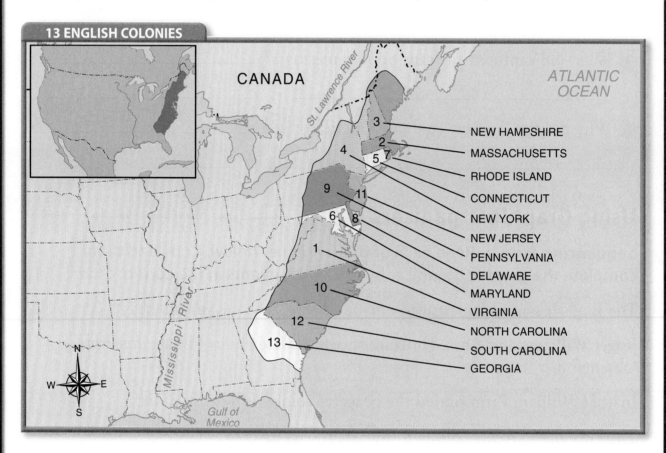

13 ENGLISH COLONIES

CANADA

ATLANTIC OCEAN

St. Lawrence River

3 — NEW HAMPSHIRE

2 — MASSACHUSETTS

4 5 7 — RHODE ISLAND

— CONNECTICUT

9 11 — NEW YORK

6 8 — NEW JERSEY

— PENNSYLVANIA

1 — DELAWARE

— MARYLAND

10 — VIRGINIA

12 — NORTH CAROLINA

13 — SOUTH CAROLINA

— GEORGIA

Mississippi River

Gulf of Mexico

N W E S

Draw a circle around each correct answer.

1 Which colony was started first?
Rhode Island   Virginia   Delaware

2 Which colony was started last?
Georgia   New York   South Carolina

3 Which colony is north of Massachusetts?
North Carolina   New Hampshire   Maryland

4 Which colony is west of New Jersey?
Connecticut   Massachusetts   Pennsylvania

NEW WORDS

shortcut
body of water
snowshoes

PEOPLE & PLACES

France
French
King Louis
Jacques Cartier
Canada
St. Lawrence River
New France
René Robert Sieur de la Salle
Gulf of Mexico
Louisiana
St. Louis
New Orleans
George Washington
North America

The French Come to America

⚡ **Learning from Pictures Who greeted these French explorers as they traveled along the St. Lawrence River?**

Many English people came to America for freedom of religion. Many poor people came to America to earn money. We learned that many Spanish people came to America to find gold. People from France also came to America. People from France are called the French.

King Louis of France wanted to find a **shortcut** to Asia. In 1534 the king sent Jacques Cartier to America. Cartier wanted to find a river in America that he could follow west all the way to Asia. Cartier sailed to Canada. He could not find a river that went to Asia. He explored the St. Lawrence River. Look at the map on page 33. Find the St. Lawrence River. Cartier said that all the land around the St. Lawrence River belonged to France. French land in America was called New France.

La Salle called the land around the Mississippi River "Louisiana." ➤

René Robert Sieur de la Salle

✐ PRIMARY SOURCE

"On either hand were vast [huge] prairies . . . hills covered with vines, fruit trees . . . and tall forest trees. . . ."

−*Father Hennepin*, who traveled with La Salle

Jacques Cartier

René Robert Sieur de la Salle also explored America for France. In 1682 La Salle traveled from the St. Lawrence River to the Mississippi River. Then he paddled a canoe down the Mississippi River to the south. In the south there is a **body of water** called the Gulf of Mexico. La Salle was the first person we know of who traveled all the way down the Mississippi River to the Gulf of Mexico.

René Robert Sieur de la Salle called the land near the Mississippi River "Louisiana." He put a big cross and a French flag on the land of Louisiana. La Salle said that Louisiana belonged to King Louis of France. The land around the Mississippi River and the land around the St. Lawrence River were part of New France.

The French started two cities on the Mississippi River. These two French cities were St. Louis and New Orleans. New Orleans was near the Gulf of Mexico.

Some French people moved to America. They came for two reasons. One reason was to get furs. Native Americans hunted animals for their furs. The French traded with the Native Americans for these furs. In France they sold these furs for a lot of money. The second reason the French came to America was to teach Native Americans how to be Catholics.

The French owned much more land in America than the English owned. But there were many more English settlers than French settlers. Few French people wanted to live in America. The French did not allow freedom of religion. Only Catholics could live in New France. So the French colony grew very slowly.

Native Americans helped the French in many ways. They taught the French how to trap animals for furs. They taught the French how to use canoes to travel on rivers. They also showed the French how to make **snowshoes**. Many parts of New France had lots of snow in the winter. When the French wore snowshoes, they could walk on very deep snow.

Native Americans had fewer fights with the French than with the Spanish or the English. The Spanish had forced Native Americans to work as slaves. The French never treated them as slaves. The English took land away from Native Americans in order to build farms and towns. The French did not take Native American lands.

French fur trapper wearing snowshoes

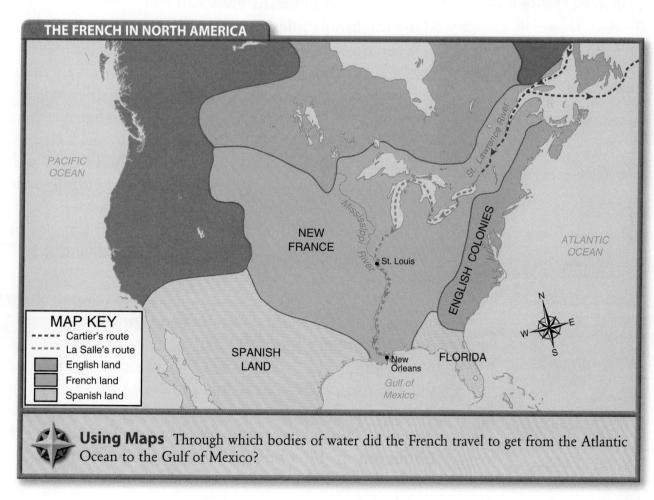

THE FRENCH IN NORTH AMERICA

PACIFIC OCEAN

NEW FRANCE

• St. Louis

Mississippi River

St. Lawrence River

ENGLISH COLONIES

ATLANTIC OCEAN

N
W E
S

MAP KEY
- - - - Cartier's route
- - - - La Salle's route
English land
French land
Spanish land

SPANISH LAND

• New Orleans

FLORIDA

Gulf of Mexico

Using Maps Through which bodies of water did the French travel to get from the Atlantic Ocean to the Gulf of Mexico?

In 1763 France lost most of its land in America when England won the French and Indian War.

England did not want France to own land in America. Many English people in the 13 colonies wanted to move west to Louisiana. France did not want English people to live in Louisiana. England and France had been enemies in Europe for many years. They became enemies in America. By 1754 England and France were fighting a war in America. This war was called the French and Indian War. Some Native Americans fought for the French, and some fought for the English. George Washington lived in the Virginia colony. He helped the English soldiers fight.

The French and the English also fought in Europe. In 1756 they began fighting in Europe. England won this war in 1763.

England also won the French and Indian War. This war ended in 1763. After the war, England owned Canada. England owned all the land that was east of the Mississippi River. Spain owned the land that was west of the Mississippi River. St. Louis and New Orleans belonged to Spain. France lost most of its land in North America. France kept two small islands in Canada and the Caribbean. In 1763 England and Spain owned most of the land in North America.

Using What You've Learned

Read and Remember

Finish the Story Use the words in blue print to finish the story. Write the words you choose on the correct blanks.

furs   Louisiana   Mississippi   canoes   Catholic   French

The French explorer La Salle traveled down the **(1)**_____ River. He paddled all the way to the Gulf of Mexico. La Salle called all the land around the Mississippi River " **(2)**_____ ." This land became part of the large French colony called New France. Some French people came to America to get **(3)**_____ . Others came to teach the **(4)**_____ religion to Native Americans. Some Native Americans taught the French how to use **(5)**_____ and snowshoes. In 1763 the **(6)**_____ lost the French and Indian War to the English.

Think and Apply

Fact or Opinion Write **F** next to each fact below. Write **O** next to each opinion. You should find four sentences that are opinions.

_____ **1** The French king wanted to find a shortcut to Asia.

_____ **2** Jacques Cartier explored the St. Lawrence River.

_____ **3** La Salle was a smarter explorer than Cartier.

_____ **4** The land around the Mississippi and St. Lawrence rivers was part of New France.

_____ **5** Before 1754 France owned more land in America than England did.

_____ **6** Only Catholics could live in New France.

_____ **7** Wearing snowshoes is the best way to walk on deep snow.

_____ **8** New France was a better place to live than in the English colonies.

_____ **9** The French were stronger soldiers than the English soldiers.

_____ **10** The French and the English fought in Europe and in America.

Skill Builder

Using Map Directions In Chapter 2 you learned that there are four main directions on a map. They are north, south, east, and west. A compass rose also shows four in-between directions. They are **northeast**, **southeast**, **northwest**, and **southwest**. Southeast is between south and east. Southwest is between south and west. Sometimes the in-between directions are shortened to **NE, SE, NW**, and **SW**.

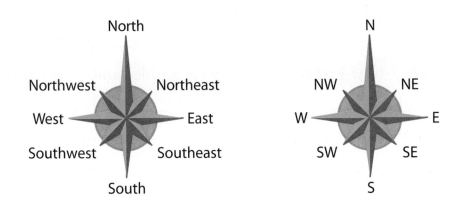

Look at the map on page 33. Then circle the word that finishes each sentence.

1 The St. Lawrence River is in the _____ .
 northeast   northwest   southwest

2 The English colonies were in the _____ .
 northwest   southwest   east

3 The Mississippi River was _____ of the English colonies.
 south   west   east

4 Florida is in the _____ .
 southeast   northeast   northwest

5 The Atlantic Ocean was to the _____ of the English colonies.
 north   west   east

6 New Orleans is in the _____ .
 northwest   northeast   south

Review

The historical map on this page shows the Spanish, French, and English colonies in North America in 1754. Study the map. Then use the words in blue print to finish the story.

Atlantic Ocean **Gulf of Mexico** **New Orleans** **Florida**

Southwest **St. Lawrence** **Jamestown** **New France**

Spain had land in the Southeast called **(1)** _____ . Spain also had land in the **(2)** _____ . Then in 1607 the English started **(3)** _____ in Virginia. All of the 13 English colonies were near the **(4)** _____ .

In 1534 Cartier explored a river in Canada called the **(5)** _____ River. La Salle traveled south on the Mississippi River to the **(6)** _____ . The French built the city of **(7)** _____ near the Gulf of Mexico. The French called their colony in America **(8)** _____ .

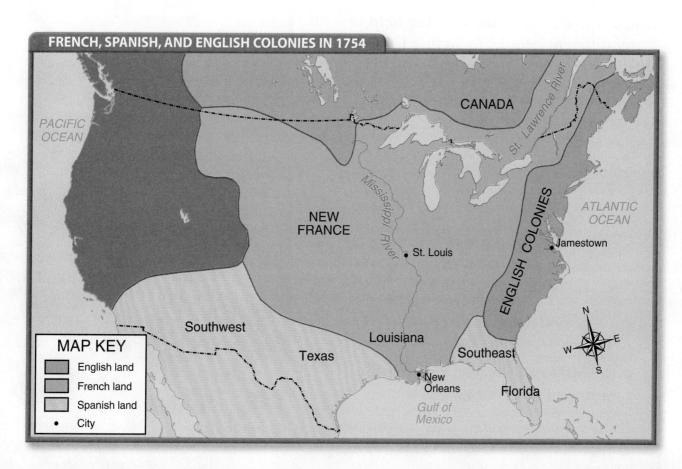

FRENCH, SPANISH, AND ENGLISH COLONIES IN 1754

PACIFIC OCEAN

CANADA

St. Lawrence River

NEW FRANCE

Mississippi River

St. Louis

ENGLISH COLONIES

ATLANTIC OCEAN

Jamestown

Southwest

Texas

Louisiana

Southeast

New Orleans

Florida

Gulf of Mexico

MAP KEY
- English land
- French land
- Spanish land
- City

Building a New Country

Imagine what it was like to live in America in 1776. Many Americans were angry at the British leaders who ruled over them. They were angry about unfair laws that the British leaders wrote for the colonies. Americans became so angry about these laws that they decided to fight for their freedom.

Americans in the 13 colonies were not ready to fight. They did not have enough guns, money, or soldiers. The British army was much stronger. How could the Americans win? It would take the help of many different people, including George Washington.

Read to Learn

- What would you have done if you had lived in 1776?
- Would you have joined the fight to make the 13 colonies a free country?
- How did Americans build a new country, the United States of America?

Americans throw tea into the Atlantic Ocean at the Boston Tea Party.
1773

1760

1770

1765
The British write the Stamp Act.

Americans write and sign the Declaration of Independence.
1776

Great Britain and America sign a peace treaty.
1783

George Washington becomes the first President of the United States.
1789

George Washington dies.
1799

1780

1790

1800

1775
The American Revolution begins.

1781
Americans win the American Revolution.

1787
Americans write the Constitution.

1791
Americans write the Bill of Rights.

1797
George Washington finishes his work as President.

39

Americans Fight for Freedom

NEW WORDS

nation
tax
Stamp Act
Parliament
port
Boston Tea Party
American Revolution

PEOPLE & PLACES

Great Britain
British
King George III
Boston

British leaders who made laws were called Parliament.

Many people from England came to live in America. They came to live in the 13 colonies. The people who lived in the colonies were called Americans. Many people came to America because they wanted more freedom.

In 1707 England and three small countries became part of a larger **nation**. The larger nation was called Great Britain. People who lived in Great Britain were called the British. Great Britain ruled the 13 American colonies. The king of Great Britain was the king of the American colonies. From 1760 to 1820, King George III was the king of Great Britain.

In 1763 the English, or British, won the French and Indian War. The war helped the American colonies. Americans felt safer because France no longer ruled Canada. Great Britain ruled Canada after this war. The British had spent a lot of

King George III

money to fight the French. The British wanted the colonies to help pay for the French and Indian War.

The British made new laws. The laws said that Americans had to send some of their money to Great Britain. The money that Americans had to send was called **tax** money. This tax money would help Great Britain get back the money it had spent on the war.

In 1765 the British made a new tax law for the colonies. It was called the **Stamp Act**. The Stamp Act said that Americans had to pay a tax on things made from paper, such as newspapers. A special stamp was placed on the newspapers to show that the tax was paid.

Americans did not like the Stamp Act. They said this tax law was unfair. It was unfair because Americans did not help make the tax law. Some Americans decided not to pay the new taxes. Some Americans burned stamps to show they were angry about the new law.

Americans wanted the same freedom to make laws that the British had. In Great Britain the British helped make their own laws. They did this by voting for leaders who would make laws for them. The British leaders who worked together to make laws for Great Britain were called **Parliament**. Americans wanted to send their own leaders to Great Britain. They wanted these leaders to be in Parliament and make laws. The British would not let Americans make laws in Parliament.

PRIMARY SOURCE

"The Revolution was in the minds and hearts of the people. This . . . change in . . . the people was the real American Revolution"

—*John Adams*

Americans burned stamps to show they did not like the Stamp Act. ▶

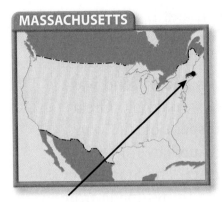

Boston

> **Learning from Pictures**
> At the Boston Tea Party, Americans threw British tea into the ocean. Why do you think people took off their hats and cheered?

Parliament wrote more tax laws for the 13 colonies. The British leaders did not let Americans help write any of these laws. Americans did not like the new laws.

In 1773 the British made another law. This law said that Americans must pay a tea tax. This meant that Americans had to pay a tax when they paid for their tea. Americans had to send the tax money to Great Britain. Americans were very angry because they did not help write the tea tax law.

Boston was a large **port** city in Massachusetts near the Atlantic Ocean. Three ships with boxes of tea came to Boston. The Americans did not want to pay a tea tax. They did not want the tea. They wanted to send the tea ships back to Great Britain. The British said that Americans had to pay for the tea.

Some Americans decided to throw the boxes of tea into the ocean. One night in 1773, they dressed up as a group of Native Americans. They went on the tea ships. The Americans threw every box of tea into the Atlantic Ocean. This is known as the **Boston Tea Party**. The Boston Tea Party made King George very angry.

▲ **The first battle of the American Revolution was in Massachusetts.**

King George punished the people of Boston. He closed Boston's port. Ships could not come to or go from the port. King George said the port would be closed until Americans paid for all the tea. The king sent many British soldiers to Massachusetts.

The British had made another law that Americans did not like. This law said that Americans must give British soldiers food and a place to sleep. The soldiers paid Americans when they ate and slept in their homes. But Americans did not like the British soldiers. They did not want the soldiers in their homes. King George sent more soldiers to Massachusetts. Americans became angrier and angrier.

The angry Americans formed an army. In 1775 America began to fight Great Britain for freedom. The fighting began in Massachusetts. The British won the first battles. But the Americans would not stop fighting. They were fighting for the same freedom that people had in Great Britain. They wanted the freedom to write their own laws. A war had started in 1775 between Great Britain and America. Americans called this war the **American Revolution**.

Using What You've Learned

Read and Remember

Match Up Finish each sentence in Group A with words from Group B. Write the letter of the correct answer on the blank line. The first one is done for you.

Group A

1. Great Britain wants the colonies to help pay for the ___c___

2. The new tax laws were not fair to Americans because _____

3. During the Boston Tea Party Americans went on three British ships and _____

4. After the Boston Tea Party, King George punished Americans by _____

5. In 1775 America began fighting a war with Great Britain that the Americans _____

Group B

a. closing the port of Boston.

b. called the American Revolution.

c. French and Indian War.

d. threw all the tea in the ocean.

e. Americans did not help write the laws in Parliament.

Think and Apply

Using Different Points of View People can look in different ways at something that happens. Look at these two points of view.

> Americans should give British soldiers food.

> British soldiers should get their own food.

In 1775 the Americans and the British had different points of view about how to rule the 13 colonies. Read each sentence below. Write **American** next to each sentence that shows the American point of view. Write **British** next to each sentence that shows the British point of view. The first sentence is done for you.

___British___ 1. Only people in Great Britain should write laws in Parliament.

_____ 2. Americans should help write their own laws in Parliament.

_____ 3. Americans should not pay a tea tax if they did not help write the tax law.

44

_____ **4** Americans should pay for all the tea they threw in the ocean.

_____ **5** Americans have enough freedom.

_____ **6** Americans should fight the British for more freedom.

Skill Builder

Reading a Time Line A **time line** is a drawing that shows years on a line. Look at this time line. Read the time line from left to right.

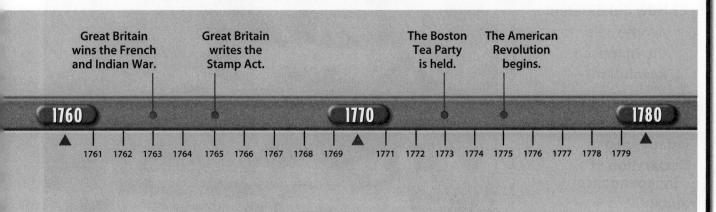

The year 1765 comes before 1766, and 1767 comes after 1766.

1 What year comes before 1775? _____

2 What year comes after 1775? _____

Events are sometimes placed on time lines. Read the events on the time line. Then answer each question.

3 When did Great Britain win the French and Indian War?

_____

4 When did Great Britain write the Stamp Act? _____

5 When was the Boston Tea Party? _____

Journal Writing

What would you do if you were an American living in the 13 colonies in 1775? Would you help the Americans or the British? Write a paragraph in your journal that tells what you would do and why.

45

A New Country Is Born

NEW WORDS

independent
Declaration of Independence
equal
Loyalists
general

PEOPLE & PLACES

Thomas Jefferson
Philadelphia
Friedrich von Steuben
Germany
Thaddeus Kosciusko
Poland
Bernardo de Gálvez
African Americans
James Armistead
Deborah Sampson
Molly Pitcher
Haym Salomon
Jewish American

In 1776 Thomas Jefferson and other leaders wrote the Declaration of Independence.

The American Revolution began in the year 1775. At first Americans were fighting the British because they wanted more freedom. American leaders wrote to King George. They asked him to let Americans write their own laws in Parliament. But King George would not give Americans more freedom. So in 1776 many Americans decided that they wanted the colonies to become **independent**. Independent means "free."

Americans decided to tell the world that the colonies no longer belonged to Great Britain. In 1776 Thomas Jefferson and four other leaders were asked to write the **Declaration of Independence**. The Declaration of Independence was an important paper. It said, "All men are created **equal**." This means that all people are just as

Thomas Jefferson was one of the writers of the Declaration of Independence.

important as a king. The Declaration said all people should have freedom. It also said that the 13 colonies were an independent nation.

The leaders of the 13 colonies met in Philadelphia in the Pennsylvania colony. On July 4, 1776, the leaders agreed to the ideas of the Declaration of Independence.

Some Americans in the colonies did not want the colonies to be free. These people were called **Loyalists**. The Loyalists fought for Great Britain during the American Revolution.

The American Revolution lasted six years. During that time George Washington was the leader of the American army. The soldiers called him **General** Washington. George Washington was a great leader. He tried to be fair to the soldiers, and he was a good fighter. The American army lost many battles, or fights. The soldiers were often hungry and cold during the winters. But General Washington did not give up. The Americans continued to fight for independence.

Many people tried to help the Americans win the war. France and Great Britain were enemies. French soldiers came to America and fought against the British.

Learning from Pictures General Washington was the leader of the American army. How were the soldiers trying to stay warm during the cold winter?

47

James Armistead

Deborah Sampson

People from other nations also helped Americans fight. Friedrich von Steuben came from Germany to help. He taught Americans how to be better soldiers. Thaddeus Kosciusko came from Poland to help Americans fight. Bernardo de Gálvez was the Spanish governor of Louisiana. He led his soldiers against the British.

All kinds of Americans fought together in the war. Farmers, sailors, business owners, and teachers all became soldiers.

About five thousand African Americans fought against the British. They fought in every important battle. James Armistead was a brave African American soldier. He was a spy for the Americans.

Women also helped win the war. They did the farm work when the men were fighting. They grew food for the soldiers. They made clothes for the army. Women also cared for soldiers who were hurt during the war. Deborah Sampson and a few other women dressed like soldiers and fought in the war.

One woman, Molly Pitcher, brought water to American soldiers when they were fighting. Molly's husband, John, was a soldier. One day John was hurt during a battle. He could not fight. Molly took John's place in the battle against the British soldiers.

Learning from Pictures How did Molly Pitcher help fight in the American Revolution?

Americans cheered for Washington and his soldiers when they won the American Revolution.

Haym Salomon

Haym Salomon was a Jewish American who helped the Americans win. He had left Poland to come to America for freedom of religion. Haym Salomon worked hard and became rich. He knew the American army had little money. The soldiers did not have enough food, clothes, or guns. Some soldiers did not even have shoes. Haym Salomon gave most of his money to the American army. The soldiers bought food, guns, shoes, and clothes with this money.

The American Revolution ended in 1781. The Americans had won. Great Britain and the colonies signed a peace treaty in 1783. People in other countries learned how the Americans won their fight for freedom. Soon people in other countries wanted more freedom, too.

After the war was over, the 13 colonies were independent. The 13 colonies became 13 states. The Americans called their new country the United States of America.

During the war, American leaders had written laws for the United States. But there were problems with those laws. In 1787 American leaders decided to write new laws for their country. In Chapter 11 you will learn how those new laws helped the nation grow.

Using Primary Sources

Diary of a Valley Forge Surgeon

Winters were very hard during the American Revolution. In the winter of 1777, George Washington and his army were at Valley Forge, Pennsylvania. The weather was snowy and very cold. There was very little food. Many of the soldiers did not even have shoes. Albigence Waldo was a surgeon, or a kind of doctor, at Valley Forge. He wrote about that hard winter. Here is part of his diary.

troops
soldiers

lame
hurt

recovered
got better

assured
made sure

December 12
... We were order'd to march over the River—It snows—I'm Sick—eat nothing. ... Cold and uncomfortable.

December 14
... The Army ... now begins to grow sickly. ... Yet they still show a spirit ... not to be expected from so young Troops. *I am Sick. ... Poor food ... Cold Weather. ... There comes a bowl of beef soup—full of burnt leaves and dirt. ... There comes a Soldier, his bare feet are seen thro' his worn out Shoes ... his Shirt hanging in Strings. ... I am Sick, my feet* lame, *my legs are sore. ...*

December 18
I have pretty well recovered. *How much better should I feel, were I* assured *my family were in health.*

On your paper, write the answer to each question.

1. What was the army ordered to do on December 12?

2. What was wrong with the soup the soldiers had on December 14?

3. Waldo wrote about a soldier on December 14. What was wrong with the soldier's clothes?

4. On what day did Waldo write that he felt better?

5. **Think and Write** Think about Waldo's diary. Why was winter at Valley Forge so hard for the soldiers?

50

Using What You've Learned

Read and Remember

Finish the Sentence Draw a circle around the date, word, or words that finish each sentence.

1 Americans in the 13 colonies told the world they were independent in
_____ .

   1765   1776   1783

2 Americans agreed to the Declaration of Independence in _____ .
Boston   Philadelphia   Jamestown

3 _____ taught Americans how to be better soldiers.
King George   Friedrich von Steuben   Molly Pitcher

4 _____ was a brave African American soldier.
Haym Salomon   James Armistead   Thomas Jefferson

5 The American Revolution ended in _____ .
1765   1776   1781

True or False Write **T** next to each sentence that is true. Write **F** next to each sentence that is false.

_____ **1** Thomas Jefferson helped write the Declaration of Independence.

_____ **2** Some Americans who fought for Great Britain during the American Revolution were called Loyalists.

_____ **3** France sent French soldiers to help the British fight.

_____ **4** Bernardo de Gálvez fought against the British.

_____ **5** Americans called their new country the United Colonies of America.

Journal Writing

Suppose that you worked for a newspaper in 1776. In your journal, write a short news story about the Declaration of Independence. Tell why Americans wrote the Declaration, and write some of the things it said.

Think and Apply

Drawing Conclusions Read the first two sentences below. Then read the third sentence. It has an idea that follows from the first two sentences. It is called a **conclusion**.

American farmers and business owners helped win the war.

Women and African Americans helped win the war.

CONCLUSION Many different Americans were important in the war.

Read each pair of sentences. Then look in the box for the conclusion you can make. Write the letter of the conclusion on the blank. The first one is done for you.

__d__ **1** American colonists wanted more freedom.
King George would not give Americans more freedom.

_____ **2** Americans called Loyalists fought for Great Britain during the American Revolution.
The Loyalists liked King George.

_____ **3** George Washington was fair to the soldiers.
George Washington lost many battles but never gave up.

_____ **4** Many women grew food and made clothes for the army.
Women took care of soldiers who were hurt.

_____ **5** Haym Salomon was a rich man.
He knew the American army needed a lot of money.

Conclusions

a. George Washington was a great army leader.

b. Haym Salomon gave money to the American army.

c. Some Americans did not want the colonies to become independent.

d. Americans decided the colonies should be independent.

e. American women helped in many ways during the war.

Benjamin Franklin

NEW WORDS

printing shop
printer
published
electric sparks
Constitution

PEOPLE & PLACES

Benjamin Franklin

➤ **Learning from Pictures** When Benjamin Franklin was a young man, he worked in his brother's printing shop. What do you think they printed?

Benjamin Franklin was born in Boston, Massachusetts, in 1706. He had 16 brothers and sisters. In those days, people used candles to light their homes. Franklin's father earned money by making soap and candles.

Ben Franklin was a smart boy. He loved to read books. He went to school until he was ten years old. Then Franklin made soap and candles with his father.

Franklin had an older brother who owned a **printing shop**. When Ben Franklin was 12 years old, he went to work for his brother. Ben Franklin became a **printer**. Franklin and his brother **published** a newspaper together. Ben Franklin enjoyed his work, but he did not like working with his brother. He decided to run away from Boston.

Philadelphia

Ben Franklin went to Philadelphia, Pennsylvania. He worked in a printing shop in Philadelphia. When Franklin was 24 years old, he published his own newspaper. People read Benjamin Franklin's newspaper in all 13 American colonies.

Ben Franklin wanted Philadelphia to be a better city. Franklin started the city's first hospital. He started a fire department. He started a school in Philadelphia. Franklin started Philadelphia's first public library.

Franklin knew there was something called electricity. He wanted to learn more about electricity. One night there were rain and lightning outside. Franklin tied a key to the end of a kite string. He flew the kite outside. Lightning hit the kite. **Electric sparks** jumped off the key. Then Ben Franklin knew that lightning is a kind of electricity. People all over America and Europe read about Ben Franklin's work with electricity. He became famous.

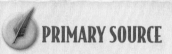

PRIMARY SOURCE

"Early to bed, early to rise, makes a man healthy, wealthy, and wise."

–*Benjamin Franklin*

Benjamin Franklin used a kite and a key to show that lightning is a kind of electricity. ➤

Benjamin Franklin

In 1765 Benjamin Franklin and many other Americans became angry about the Stamp Act. Franklin traveled to Great Britain. He spoke to Parliament about the Stamp Act. He told the British why the tax law was not fair. Soon after that, the Stamp Act ended.

Franklin thought the American colonies should be an independent country. He helped Thomas Jefferson write the Declaration of Independence in 1776. He was one of the men who signed the Declaration. Franklin wanted to help his country win the American Revolution. He was then seventy years old. Franklin went to France. He asked the French people to help the Americans fight. France sent soldiers and ships to the American colonies. France helped the Americans win the war.

In 1787 Ben Franklin was 81 years old. He helped write new laws for his country. The new laws were called the **Constitution**. Franklin and the other leaders spent four months writing the Constitution in Philadelphia.

Benjamin Franklin died in Philadelphia when he was 84 years old. He helped Philadelphia become a great city. He helped the United States become a free country.

Benjamin Franklin went to France to get help for the American soldiers. ➤

Using What You've Learned

Read and Remember

Find the Answers Put a check (√) next to each sentence below that tells how Benjamin Franklin helped Philadelphia and America. You should check four sentences.

_____ **1** Benjamin Franklin was born in Boston in 1706.

_____ **2** Franklin started a hospital and a public library in Philadelphia.

_____ **3** Franklin started a fire department in Philadelphia.

_____ **4** Franklin helped Thomas Jefferson write the Declaration of Independence.

_____ **5** Franklin was about seventy years old during the American Revolution.

_____ **6** Franklin helped write the Constitution in 1787.

Using Graphic Organizers

Cause and Effect Read each of the sentences under cause below. Then read each of the sentences under effect. Copy and then complete the graphic organizer to match each cause on the left with an effect on the right.

Cause

1 Franklin learned how to be a printer in Boston, so _____

2 Lightning hit Franklin's kite and sparks flew off the key, so _____

3 Franklin wanted the American colonies to become independent, so _____

Effect

a. he signed the Declaration of Independence.

b. Franklin learned that lightning is a kind of electricity.

c. he found a job as a printer in Philadelphia.

Cause		Effect
1.	→	
2.	→	
3.	→	

56

Skill Builder

Reading a Bar Graph **Graphs** are drawings that help you compare facts. The graph on this page is a **bar graph**. It uses bars of different lengths to show facts. The bar graph below shows the **population** of America's three largest cities in 1776. The number of people in a city is its population.

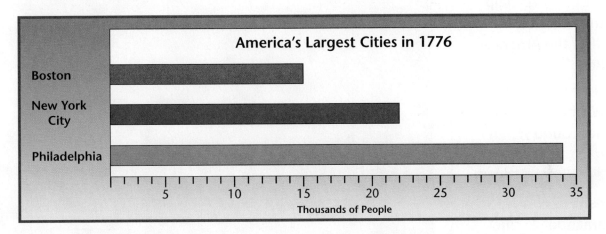

Use the bar graph to answer each question. Draw a circle around the correct answer.

1. How many people lived in Boston in 1776?
   15,000   22,000   34,000

2. How many people lived in Philadelphia in 1776?
   15,000   22,000   34,000

3. What was the population of New York City in 1776?
   5,000   10,000   22,000

4. Which city had the largest population in 1776?
   Boston   New York City   Philadelphia

5. Which of these three cities had the smallest population in 1776?
   Boston   New York City   Philadelphia

Journal Writing

In your journal, write a paragraph telling why Benjamin Franklin was so important in American history.

George Washington

Many Americans call George Washington the "Father of Our Country."

George Washington was born in the Virginia colony on February 22, 1732. His parents owned a large house with a lot of farmland. George Washington was a quiet, shy boy. His father died when he was 11 years old. Washington then helped his mother **manage** the family farm. He learned how to be a good farmer.

George Washington was a soldier in Virginia. He was tall and strong. In 1754 Great Britain and France began fighting the French and Indian War. Washington became a leader of the Virginia army. He was 22 years old. Washington and the Americans helped the British win the war.

Martha Washington

George and Martha Washington lived at Mount Vernon in Virginia.

In 1759 George Washington married a wealthy woman named Martha. They lived in a large, beautiful house in Virginia. They called their home Mount Vernon. There were large farms at Mount Vernon. Washington loved to manage his farms.

In 1775 the American Revolution began. George Washington wanted the American colonies to become independent. He became the **commander in chief** of the American army. This means that he was the leader of all the American soldiers. The soldiers called him General Washington.

General Washington lost a battle in New York City, New York. But he did not give up. He took his army south to Pennsylvania. On Christmas 1776 Washington took his army to Trenton, New Jersey. Find Trenton on the map on page 60. Washington knew that the British army there would be having Christmas parties. They would not be ready to fight. Washington's army surprised the British army. The British army **surrendered**. General Washington won the Battle of Trenton, but the war was not over.

The British and the Americans continued to fight. The American army did not have enough food, clothes, or guns. Many soldiers became sick during the cold winters. Most soldiers liked George Washington. They stayed with him and helped him fight for American freedom.

New York City
Trenton
Yorktown

KEY
Battle site

Important battles

In 1781 British soldiers surrendered to General Washington in Yorktown, Virginia.

Martha Washington helped the American army during the war. Martha stayed with George during the six cold winters of the American Revolution. She sewed clothes for the soldiers. She fixed their torn shirts and pants. Martha took care of soldiers who became sick or hurt.

In 1781 the Americans won an important battle at Yorktown, Virginia. There the British army surrendered to George Washington. The American Revolution was over. In 1783 Great Britain and the colonies signed a peace treaty. Then General Washington said goodbye to the army. He was ready to go home to Mount Vernon.

Soon the American people needed George Washington again. They wanted him to help write the Constitution. In 1787 American leaders met in Philadelphia to write new laws for the United States. These meetings were called the **Constitutional Convention**. Washington became president of the Constitutional Convention. He helped the leaders work together to write laws. After that he wanted to return to Mount Vernon. But Americans voted for George Washington to be the new country's first President.

Learning from Pictures In 1789 George Washington became the first President of the United States. What do you think he is doing in this picture?

Benjamin Banneker

George Washington became our President in 1789. Martha Washington became the **First Lady**. The government of the United States was in New York City. So George and Martha Washington left Mount Vernon. They traveled to New York City. Washington was America's hero. As he traveled, crowds everywhere cheered for him.

American leaders wanted the United States to have a new capital city. Washington found a beautiful place for the capital between Maryland and Virginia. He asked a Frenchman named Pierre L'Enfant to plan the new city.

Benjamin Banneker, a free African American, helped L'Enfant plan the new city. Banneker knew a lot about math and science. He used math and science to help plan the **boundaries** of the new capital. Banneker also wrote to American leaders about ending slavery in the new country. In 1800 the government moved to the new capital. The capital is now called Washington, D.C.

George Washington was President for eight years. As President, George Washington helped the United States become a stronger nation. In 1797 Washington returned to Mount Vernon. He died at his home in 1799.

George Washington was one of our greatest American leaders. He led our country in war and in peace. Many people call him the "Father of Our Country."

Using Geography Themes

Location: Washington, D.C.

The theme of **location** tells where a place is found. Sometimes people use directions to tell where a place is. People also can say what the place is near or what is around it.

Read the paragraphs about Washington, D.C. Study the photo below and the map on page 63.

After the American Revolution, American leaders decided the United States needed a capital city. The leaders of the United States government would work in the new capital.

In 1790 the leaders decided the capital would be in a southern area of the United States. They wanted the new city to be on the Potomac River. This river flows between Maryland and Virginia. Ships could sail from the Atlantic Ocean into Chesapeake Bay. From the bay, ships could sail on the Potomac River to the new capital. President George Washington picked the area on the Potomac River for the capital city.

Washington, D.C., is not part of any state. It is on land between Maryland and Virginia. The land belongs to the United States government. After George Washington died, the capital was named Washington, D.C. It has been the capital of the United States since 1800.

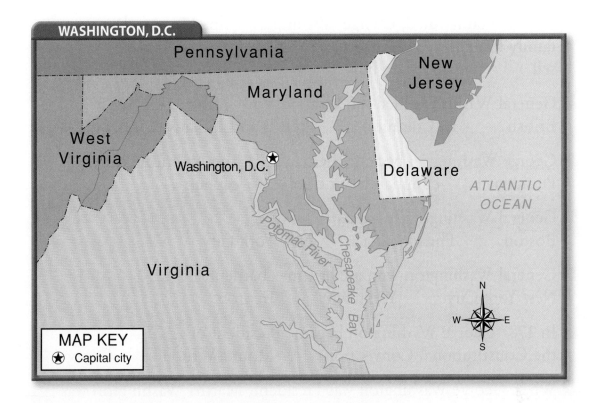

On your paper, write the answer to each question.

1 Look at the map. Between what two states is Washington, D.C., the nation's capital?

2 Along what river is Washington, D.C.?

3 What state is just to the north of Washington, D.C.?

4 What bay leads to the Potomac River?

5 Do you travel north or south to get from Pennsylvania to Washington, D.C.?

6 What are three ways to describe where Washington, D.C., is located?

Using What You've Learned

Read and Remember

Finish the Sentence Draw a circle around the word or words that finish each sentence.

1. After his father died, George Washington helped his mother _____ the family farm.
   sell   manage   buy

2. General Washington led the Virginia army in the _____ War.
   British   13 Colonies'   French and Indian

3. George Washington became the _____ of the American army.
   President   commander in chief   captain

4. General Washington lost a battle in _____ .
   Boston   Philadelphia   New York City

5. General Washington won a Christmas battle in _____ .
   New York City   Yorktown   Trenton

6. In 1787 George Washington became president of _____ .
   the Constitutional Convention   Mount Vernon   Georgia

7. When George Washington was President, Martha Washington was _____ .
   general   First Lady   commander in chief

8. Pierre L'Enfant and _____ planned the capital city of Washington, D.C.
   Benjamin Franklin   James Armistead   Benjamin Banneker

Think and Apply

Sequencing Events Write the numbers 1, 2, 3, 4, and 5 next to these sentences to show the correct order.

_____ George Washington became the first President of the United States.

_____ Washington helped the British win the French and Indian War.

_____ The British army surrendered to George Washington in Yorktown.

_____ George Washington helped write the Constitution.

_____ General Washington led the American army during the American Revolution.

The Constitution

➤ **Learning from Pictures Many leaders met together to write the United States Constitution. What do you think their meetings were like?**

The American Revolution was won in 1781. The United States was an independent country with 13 states. American leaders had written laws for the country. But there were problems with these first laws. The leaders decided to write a new constitution. In 1787 leaders from 12 of the states went to Philadelphia. There they wrote the United States Constitution at the Constitutional Convention.

Before the American Revolution, Great Britain made laws for the 13 colonies. Americans liked the way the British voted for leaders to write laws in Parliament. The United States leaders planned the Constitution so that Americans could help write their own laws. How do Americans do this?

The United States Constitution in 1787

The Constitution says that Americans should choose, or vote for, people to work for them in their government. Our country's laws are made by men and women in **Congress**. In some ways our Congress is like Great Britain's Parliament. Americans vote for people who will make laws for them in Congress. There are two houses, or parts, of Congress. The **Senate** and the **House of Representatives** are the two houses of Congress.

Men and women who write laws are called **senators** and **representatives**. Every state sends two senators to work in the Senate. States with many people send many representatives to work in the House of Representatives. States with fewer people send fewer representatives to work in the House of Representatives. The senators and representatives meet in a building called the Capitol. The Constitution says that Americans should vote for people to be their senators and representatives. Americans help write their own laws by voting for their senators and representatives.

Congress writes laws in the Capitol building in Washington, D.C. The two houses of Congress are the Senate and the House of Representatives.

Bill of Rights in 1791

The White House

The Constitution says the President should carry out the country's laws. Americans vote for a President every four years. The President also helps make our laws. The White House is where the President lives and works.

The Constitution also gives the United States its **Supreme Court**. Nine **justices**, or judges, work in the Supreme Court. The Supreme Court justices decide whether our laws agree with the Constitution.

The White House, the Capitol, and the Supreme Court buildings are in the city of Washington, D.C. Important government leaders live and work in the capital city.

Together Congress, the President, and the Supreme Court make up the three **branches of government**. The Constitution gives our country these three branches. Each branch has separate powers. Congress is the branch with the power to write laws. The President leads the branch that has the power to carry out the laws. The Supreme Court is the branch that decides whether the laws agree with the Constitution.

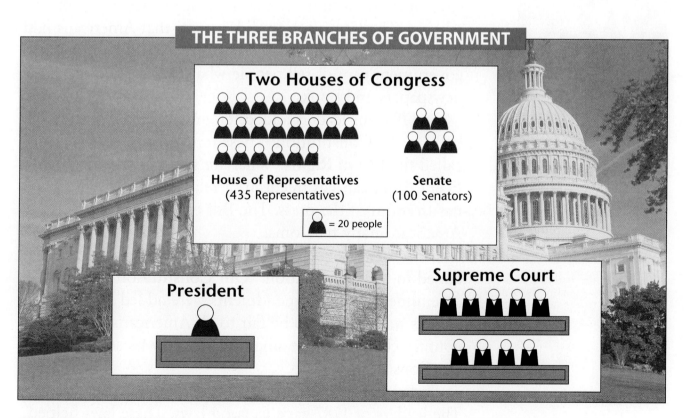

THE THREE BRANCHES OF GOVERNMENT

Two Houses of Congress

House of Representatives
(435 Representatives)

Senate
(100 Senators)

= 20 people

President

Supreme Court

Congress, the President, and the Supreme Court work together in the government.

The President sometimes meets with all the senators and representatives of Congress in the Capitol building.

An American voting

Some of our leaders were not happy with the Constitution when it was written in 1787. The Constitution did not say that Americans had freedom of religion. The Constitution did not say that Americans had **freedom of the press**. "Freedom of the press" means the government cannot tell people what they can say in newspapers and books.

In 1791 our leaders added ten **amendments**, or new laws, to the Constitution. These ten amendments are called the **Bill of Rights**. What are some of these rights? Every American has freedom of religion. Every American has freedom of the press. The Bill of Rights gives every American many freedoms.

Since 1791, seventeen more amendments have been added to the Constitution. Our Constitution now has 27 amendments. These amendments were added because our leaders wanted laws to be fair to all Americans. As our country changes, more amendments may be added to the Constitution.

Today our Constitution is more than 200 years old. The leaders of 1787 gave us good laws. These laws helped the United States become a great country.

Using What You've Learned

Read and Remember

Write the Answer Write one or more sentences to answer each question.

1. Where did American leaders write the Constitution? _____

   _____

2. What do senators and representatives do in Congress? _____

   _____

3. How many senators does each state have in the United States Senate? _____

   _____

4. What does the President do? _____

   _____

Using Graphic Organizers

Main Idea and Supporting Details Read each group of sentences below.
One of the three sentences is a main idea. The other two sentences support
the main idea. Copy the chart three times. Then complete one chart for each
group of sentences.

1. Before the American Revolution, Great Britain made laws for the colonies.
   Americans made a constitution that said they could help write their
   own laws.
   Americans wanted to help write their own laws.

2. The Constitution says Americans can choose people to work in their
   government.
   Americans vote for their senators and representatives.
   Americans vote for their President every four years.

3. The President and the Supreme Court are two branches of the United States
   government.
   The Senate and the House of Representatives make up one branch of the
   United States government.
   The United States government has three branches.

Main Idea

Detail	Detail

Skill Builder

Reading a Diagram A **diagram** is a picture that helps you understand information. The diagram on page 67 helps you understand our government. Look back at the diagram. Then finish each sentence with a word in blue print.

President	nine	435
senators	three	100

1. The United States government has _____ branches.

2. The government has one _____ .

3. The government has _____ Supreme Court justices.

4. There are fewer _____ than representatives.

5. There are _____ members of the House of Representatives.

6. There are _____ members of the Senate.

Journal Writing

After the American Revolution, Americans wanted their new Constitution to say that people could help write their own laws. Write a paragraph in your journal that explains how early American leaders set up our government so that Americans could help write laws.

Review

The historical map on this page shows the United States in 1800. Study the map. Then use the words in blue print to finish the story.

Yorktown	**Philadelphia**	**Boston**
New York City	**Washington, D.C.**	**Trenton**

Americans were angry when the British said they had to pay a tax on tea. So Americans in **(1)** _____ threw tea into the Atlantic Ocean. In 1776 Americans signed the Declaration of Independence in **(2)** _____ .

During the American Revolution, George Washington won a Christmas battle at **(3)** _____ . In 1781 the British army surrendered to Washington at **(4)** _____ . In 1789 Washington went to **(5)** _____ to become the first President. As President he planned the country's new capital. The name of the capital is **(6)** _____ . American leaders live and work in the capital city.

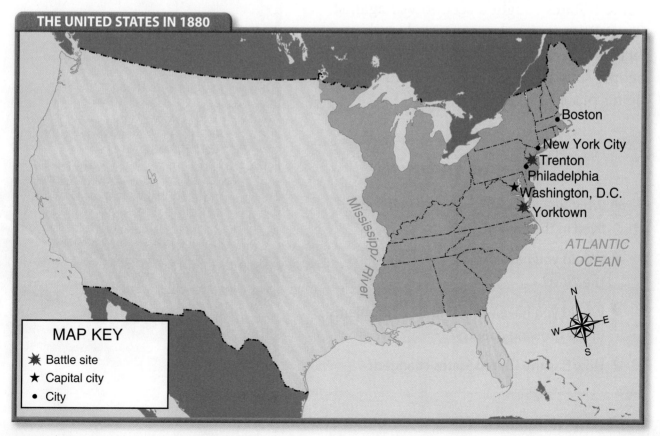

THE UNITED STATES IN 1880

Boston
New York City
Trenton
Philadelphia
Washington, D.C.
Yorktown

ATLANTIC OCEAN

Mississippi River

MAP KEY
✳ Battle site
★ Capital city
• City

The United States Grows

Thomas Jefferson becomes the third President.
1801

Lewis and Clark explore Louisiana.
1804

1800 ● ● ● 1810

▲

1803
The United States buys New Orleans and Louisiana.

Suppose you were an explorer in the year 1803. The United States had bought a large piece of land west of the Mississippi River. President Thomas Jefferson had decided to send people to explore it. Your trip would be long and slow. You would cross mountains and rivers. You would meet many groups of Native Americans.

There were many changes in the United States in the early 1800s. The country became much larger. From 1812 to 1814, the United States fought a second war against Great Britain. Americans started working in factories. American cities grew larger. Many people worked to make the United States a better place to live.

Read to Learn

- What would you have done if you had lived in the early 1800s?

- Would you have explored new lands in the West?

- Would you have worked to solve problems in the growing country?

- How has the United States changed?

The War of 1812 begins.
1812

Sequoyah makes the first Native American alphabet.
1821

Andrew Jackson becomes President.
1829

Elizabeth Cady Stanton holds a meeting for women's rights.
1848

1820

1830

1840

1850

1814
Great Britain and the United States sign a peace treaty to end the war.

1825
The Erie Canal is completed.

1837
Mount Holyoke Female Seminary opens.

1838
The Cherokee are forced to move west.

NEW WORDS

crops
Louisiana Purchase
doubled

PEOPLE & PLACES

West
Napoleon Bonaparte
Meriwether Lewis
William Clark
York
Rocky Mountains
Pacific Ocean
Sacagawea

The United States Doubles in Size

➤ **Learning from Pictures A Shoshone Indian woman named Sacagawea helped Lewis and Clark travel to the Pacific Ocean. Why do you think Lewis and Clark needed Sacagawea's help?**

The man who wrote most of the Declaration of Independence became President of the United States in 1801. Americans voted for Thomas Jefferson to be their third President.

The American Revolution was over. The United States owned all the land east of the Mississippi River except Florida. At first, most Americans lived in the 13 states near the Atlantic Ocean. But every year more Americans moved to the West. By 1800 almost one million Americans lived on the land between the 13 states and the Mississippi River. They built homes and farms. They started new states for the United States. In 1803 the United States had 17 states.

Thomas Jefferson

Napoleon Bonaparte

The United States bought New Orleans from France as part of the Louisiana Purchase in 1803.

Sometimes Americans moved to land that was being used by Native Americans. There were fights between Indian nations and settlers about who would use the land. Many Native Americans, were forced off their land.

New Orleans was an important port city near the Gulf of Mexico and the Mississippi River. Many American farmers lived near the Mississippi River. They sent their farm **crops** in boats down the Mississippi River to New Orleans. American farmers sold their farm crops in New Orleans. Ships from New Orleans carried the crops to port cities on the Atlantic Ocean.

Spain owned Louisiana and the city of New Orleans. You read about Louisiana in Chapter 6. Spain allowed American ships to use the port of New Orleans. In 1800 Spain gave New Orleans and Louisiana back to France. New Orleans was a French city again. President Jefferson was worried. Perhaps France would not allow Americans to use the port.

President Jefferson knew that American farmers needed the port of New Orleans. He wanted the United States to own New Orleans. Thomas Jefferson decided to offer to buy the city from France.

Napoleon Bonaparte was the ruler of France. France was fighting many wars in Europe. Napoleon needed

UNDER MY WINGS EVERY THING PROSPERS

Clark's journal

money for the French wars. Jefferson asked Napoleon to sell New Orleans to the United States. Napoleon said he would sell New Orleans and all of Louisiana to the United States. In 1803 the United States paid $15 million for Louisiana. Look at the map of the **Louisiana Purchase** on this page. The United States now owned New Orleans and much land to the west of the Mississippi River. The United States **doubled** in size in 1803.

President Jefferson wanted to learn about the land, plants, and animals of Louisiana. He wanted to know about the many Indian nations who lived on this land. Jefferson asked Meriwether Lewis to explore Louisiana. Lewis asked William Clark to explore the new land with him. They formed a group with about 42 men.

Lewis and Clark started their trip across Louisiana in 1804. During the trip Lewis and Clark kept journals. They wrote about the people, plants, animals, and mountains.

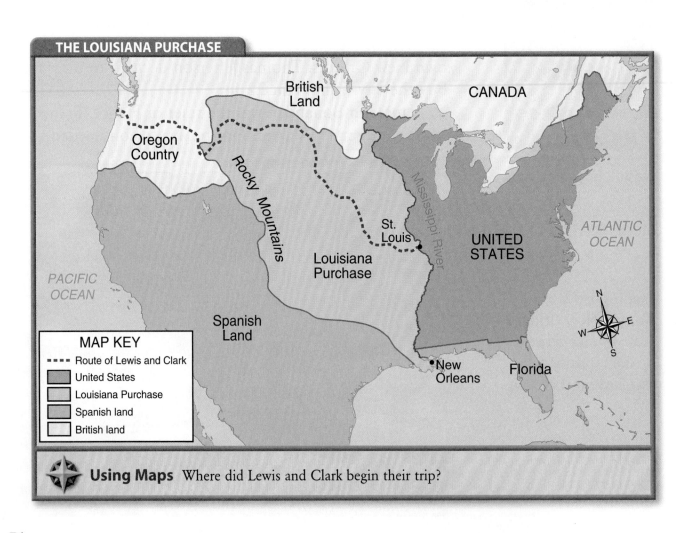

THE LOUISIANA PURCHASE

British Land

CANADA

Oregon Country

Rocky Mountains

St. Louis

Mississippi River

UNITED STATES

ATLANTIC OCEAN

PACIFIC OCEAN

Louisiana Purchase

Spanish Land

New Orleans

Florida

MAP KEY
- - - - Route of Lewis and Clark
United States
Louisiana Purchase
Spanish land
British land

Using Maps Where did Lewis and Clark begin their trip?

Sacagawea and York help Lewis and Clark get along with Native Americans. ➤

An African American named York traveled with Lewis and Clark. York was Clark's slave. He was a good hunter. York helped Lewis and Clark explore the west. Sometime after the trip ended, Clark gave York his freedom.

During their trip Lewis and Clark reached the tall Rocky Mountains. They wanted to cross these mountains and go to the Pacific Ocean. A Shoshone Indian woman told Lewis and Clark that she could help them cross the Rocky Mountains. Her name was Sacagawea. She was about 17 years old. Sacagawea said Lewis and Clark needed horses to cross the mountains. She helped them trade with the Shoshone for horses.

Sacagawea and her husband led the group across the Rocky Mountains. Sacagawea had a baby boy. She carried the baby on her back. She helped the men find food. The trip across the mountains was slow and dangerous. After many months, the group traveled west to the Pacific Ocean. The map on page 76 shows their route. In 1806 Lewis, Clark, and Sacagawea returned to their homes. They had explored 8,000 miles of land in the West.

Lewis and Clark told Thomas Jefferson about the land they had explored. They made new maps of the West. Thomas Jefferson helped the United States double in size. York, Sacagawea, Lewis, and Clark helped Americans learn about the land in the West.

Using What You've Learned

Read and Remember

True or False Write **T** next to each sentence that is true. Write **F** next to each sentence that is false.

_____ **1)** After the American Revolution, the United States owned all the land east of the Mississippi River.

_____ **2)** Few Americans moved west to the land between the first 13 states and the Mississippi River.

_____ **3)** New Orleans was an important port for American farmers.

_____ **4)** Spain gave Louisiana back to France in 1800.

_____ **5)** Napoleon Bonaparte did not want to sell Louisiana to the United States.

_____ **6)** The United States paid $15 million for Louisiana and New Orleans.

_____ **7)** York and Sacagawea helped Lewis and Clark explore the West.

Skill Builder

Reviewing Map Directions Study the map on page 76. Choose a word in blue print to finish each sentence. Write the word on the correct blank.

east	south	northwest
west	north	southeast

1) The Pacific Ocean is _____ of the Rocky Mountains.

2) Canada is _____ of the United States.

3) Before the Louisiana Purchase, most Americans lived _____ of the Mississippi River.

4) New Orleans was _____ of the United States.

5) Oregon Country was in the _____ .

6) Florida was _____ of Oregon Country.

Think and Apply

Categories Read the words in each group. Decide how they are alike. Find the best title in blue print for each group. Write the title on the line above each group.

Lewis and Clark   **Napoleon Bonaparte**
Jefferson   **Louisiana**

1 _____

wrote most of the Declaration of Independence
third President of the United States
wanted the United States to buy Louisiana from France

2 _____

ruler of France
wanted to sell Louisiana
needed money for wars in Europe

3 _____

west of the Mississippi River
had the port city of New Orleans
doubled the size of the United States

4 _____

explored Louisiana
kept journals
made maps of the West

Journal Writing

Look at the list below. If you had gone with Lewis and Clark, which things would you have taken? Choose the five things you think are most important. In your journal, write a paragraph telling why you would have taken each one.

axe	rope	journal	matches	candles
soap	knife	blanket	animal trap	hat

The War of 1812

➤ **Learning from Pictures Americans fought the British in the War of 1812 for freedom of the seas. Which ship won this battle at sea?**

The United States and Great Britain were fighting again in the year 1812. Why did Americans fight a second war against the British?

Napoleon Bonaparte, the ruler of France, started a war against Great Britain in 1803. The United States wanted to trade with both Great Britain and France. British ships **captured** many American ships that sailed to France. The French did the same thing to ships that sailed to Great Britain. This made Americans very angry. Americans wanted **freedom of the seas**. "Freedom of the seas" means that ships can sail wherever they want.

The British angered Americans in another way. British ships stopped American ships on the ocean. British captains

James Madison

Tecumseh

went on the American ships. These captains said that many of the Americans were really British people. They forced these Americans to sail on the British ships. The British made many Americans work for the British **navy**. Americans wanted to trade with France. They did not want their ships captured.

The French agreed to freedom of the seas. The British did not. In 1812 the United States began to fight Great Britain for freedom of the seas. This second war against Great Britain was called the War of 1812. James Madison was President during the War of 1812. He thought the United States would win the war quickly. But the American army and navy were small. The war did not end quickly. Americans fought against the British for more than two years.

During the War of 1812, the United States tried to capture Canada. Canada belonged to Great Britain. The British army in Canada was strong. The United States could not capture Canada.

A Native American leader named Tecumseh fought for the British during the War of 1812. Tecumseh lived on land between the eastern states and the Mississippi River.

▲ **Tecumseh was killed in a battle during the War of 1812.**

81

Dolley Madison

Dolley Madison saved important papers when the British marched into Washington, D.C. ▶

He was angry because each year Americans took more land that belonged to Native Americans. The British promised Tecumseh that they would help the Native Americans get back their land. So Tecumseh and his people fought for Great Britain. He helped them win some battles in Canada. Tecumseh was killed in a battle during the War of 1812.

The American army had burned some buildings in Canada. The British army decided to burn the American capital city, Washington, D.C. President Madison was not in the city when the British army arrived.

Dolley Madison, the First Lady, was in the White House when Washington, D.C., began to burn. The brave First Lady stayed in the White House. She packed important government papers in a trunk. A famous painting of George Washington was in the White House. Dolley Madison left the burning city with the painting and the government papers. Very soon, British soldiers came to the White House and burned everything still inside. Dolley Madison had saved the painting of Washington and the government papers for the United States.

Andrew Jackson and his soldiers won the Battle of New Orleans. ➤

THE WAR OF 1812

CANADA

Washington, D.C.

MAP KEY
★ Battle site

New Orleans

Important battles

In 1814 the British tried to capture Fort McHenry. This fort guarded the port of Baltimore, Maryland. A large American flag flew over the fort. After the battle, an American named Francis Scott Key saw that this flag still flew over the fort. The flag showed that Americans had won the battle. Francis Scott Key wrote a song about the flag. His song was called "The Star-Spangled Banner." It became our country's song.

The British wanted to capture the port of New Orleans. Andrew Jackson was a general in the American army. He led 5,000 American soldiers in the Battle of New Orleans. These soldiers included people from Europe, Native Americans, slaves, and free African Americans. General Jackson won the Battle of New Orleans in January 1815. He did not know that the war had ended already. In December 1814 Great Britain and the United States had signed a peace treaty.

Nothing really changed much because of the War of 1812. Neither country won new land in the war. But Great Britain never again fought against the United States. Great Britain and other countries now knew that the United States was strong enough to fight for what it wanted.

83

Using Primary Sources

Chief Tecumseh's Speech, 1810

There were many groups of Native Americans that lived on land between the states and the Mississippi River. In the early 1800s, many of these groups were forced to sign treaties with Governor William Henry Harrison. In these treaties, Native Americans gave their land to the United States.

Tecumseh was the chief of the Shawnee, a group of Native Americans. He was very angry about the treaties. In 1810 Tecumseh met with Governor Harrison. Tecumseh told Harrison that the United States had no right to take land from Native Americans. Here is part of his speech.

Great Spirit important Native American god

race people

miserable unhappy

unite join together

> *Once . . . there was no white man on this continent. . . . All belonged to red men, children of the same parents, placed on it by the **Great Spirit** that made them, to keep it . . . , and to fill it with the same **race**. Once a happy race—since made **miserable** by the white people. . . . The way . . . to stop this evil is for all the red men to **unite** in claiming a common and equal right in the land . . . ; for it . . . belongs to all. . . .*
>
> *The white people have no right to take the land from the Indians, because they had it first; it is theirs. . . . All red men have equal rights to the . . . land. . . . It belongs to the first who sits down on his blanket or skins which he has thrown upon the ground; and till he leaves it, no other has a right.*

On your paper, write the answer to each question.

1 Who was Tecumseh?

2 To whom did Tecumseh give his speech in 1810?

3 What god did Tecumseh believe placed Native Americans on the land?

4 Who did Tecumseh say made Native Americans unhappy?

5 **Think and Write** How does Tecumseh describe life before Americans arrived? Why might Tecumseh believe that he and other Native Americans own the land they live on?

Using What You've Learned

Read and Remember

Choose the Answer Draw a circle around the correct answer.

1. What country was Great Britain fighting in 1803?
   the United States   France   Spain

2. What did the United States fight Great Britain for in 1812?
   freedom of the seas   freedom of the press   freedom of religion

3. Who was President during the War of 1812?
   George Washington   Thomas Jefferson   James Madison

4. Who fought for Great Britain during the War of 1812?
   Tecumseh   Andrew Jackson   James Madison

5. What did Tecumseh want?
   to be rich   to get back Native American lands   to go to France

6. Who saved the painting of George Washington when the British burned Washington, D.C.?
   Dolley Madison   Molly Pitcher   Martha Washington

7. Which country won the battle at Fort McHenry?
   the United States   Great Britain   France

8. Who wrote our country's song, "The Star-Spangled Banner"?
   a British soldier   Francis Scott Key   Dolley Madison

9. Who won the Battle of New Orleans?
   James Armistead   Benjamin Franklin   Andrew Jackson

Journal Writing

It often took months for mail to get anywhere in the United States. Because of the slow mail, Andrew Jackson didn't know that the War of 1812 had ended. He and his soldiers fought the Battle of New Orleans. Imagine how he felt when he learned that the peace treaty had already been signed. Write four or five sentences in your journal that tell how Jackson must have felt.

Think and Apply

Drawing Conclusions Read each pair of sentences. Then look in the box for the conclusion you can make. Write the letter of the conclusion on the blank.

1 British ships captured American ships that were sailing to France.
British captains forced American sailors to work on British ships.

Conclusion _____

2 African Americans fought in the United States Army.
People from Europe fought for the United States.

Conclusion _____

3 Great Britain and the United States wanted peace.
Both countries had won and lost many battles.

Conclusion _____

4 In December 1814 Great Britain and the United States signed a peace treaty.
In January 1815 Andrew Jackson won the Battle of New Orleans.

Conclusion _____

Conclusions

a. Great Britain and the United States signed a peace treaty.

b. Americans wanted freedom of the seas.

c. Andrew Jackson did not know that the war was over.

d. Many people helped the United States in the War of 1812.

The Industrial Revolution

NEW WORDS

invented
Industrial Revolution
goods
cotton gin
mass production
steamboat
steam engine
canals
locomotives

PEOPLE & PLACES

Samuel Slater
Eli Whitney
Francis Cabot Lowell
Robert Fulton
Hudson River
Erie Canal
Lake Erie

➤ **Learning from Pictures** During the Industrial Revolution, how might factory machines have been dangerous for workers?

In the 1700s most people wore clothes that were made by hand. They wore shoes that were made by hand, too. Then in the late 1700s the British **invented** machines to help them make cloth. Soon the British began to use the machines in factories. This was the start of the **Industrial Revolution**. The Industrial Revolution began in Great Britain.

The Industrial Revolution was different from the American Revolution. The Industrial Revolution was a change in the way **goods** were made. Before this revolution, most goods were made by hand at home. After the revolution began, machines in factories made many goods.

In 1790 the Industrial Revolution began in the United States. It brought many changes to American life.

Samuel Slater

Eli Whitney

Eli Whitney's cotton gin removed seeds from cotton quickly.

Samuel Slater helped start the Industrial Revolution in the United States. Slater had grown up in Great Britain. He studied how the British built their machines for making cloth. Then he moved to the United States. He built new machines for spinning thread. In 1790 Slater and a partner built a factory where workers could use Slater's spinning machines. Soon the factory was making lots of thread.

Eli Whitney also changed the way goods were made. In 1793 Whitney invented a machine called the **cotton gin**. This machine helped cotton farmers. After cotton was picked, seeds had to be removed from the cotton plant. Before the cotton gin, workers removed the seeds by hand. After all the seeds were removed, cotton could be made into thread. It took a long time to remove the cotton seeds by hand. The new cotton gin removed the seeds quickly. Farmers began to grow much more cotton. The cotton was made into thread in factories.

Eli Whitney helped the Industrial Revolution in another way. He began **mass production**. In mass production, people or machines make many goods that are exactly alike. In 1798 the United States Army needed many new guns. Whitney showed how he could use his machines to make thousands of guns in one factory. All the guns were alike. They had the same parts. If a part for

one gun broke, the gun could be fixed with the same part for another gun. Soon many factories began using mass production. It became faster and cheaper to make goods.

Francis Cabot Lowell started a factory for making cloth in Massachusetts. Lowell was the first person to put all the machines for making thread and cloth in one factory. He needed workers for his factory. He hired young women to work in his factory. Lowell tried to give his workers good places to live. But the women had to work very hard. They had to work with dangerous machines. They worked in the factory from morning until night. Many other factories hired both women and children.

Most American factories were built near rivers. Water power from the rivers was used to run the machines. The rivers also were used to move factory goods from one place to another. Ships carried goods on rivers to many parts of the country.

People wanted to travel faster on rivers. In 1807 a man named Robert Fulton sailed a **steamboat** on the Hudson River in New York. A **steam engine** helped the boat move faster. By the 1820s there were many steamboats carrying people and goods on rivers.

▲ **In 1807 Robert Fulton sailed his steamboat, the Clermont, up the Hudson River.**

The Erie Canal helped ships travel all the way from the Atlantic Ocean to Lake Erie. ➤

Locomotive pulling train

Soon Americans needed more waterways to move goods. They began to build **canals**. These canals were waterways that joined rivers and lakes. The first big canal was built in New York. It was the Erie Canal. It was finished in 1825. Ships sailed from the Atlantic Ocean into the port of New York City. Then they sailed up the Hudson River. From there ships could sail on the Erie Canal all the way to Lake Erie. The canal was more than 350 miles long. Many new businesses, factories, and cities were built near the Erie Canal. The canal helped New York City become a very large city.

People wanted a better way to travel across land. Wagons were very slow. People began to build railroads. At first, horses pulled the trains. Soon people wanted faster trains. They built trains that were pulled by **locomotives**. Each locomotive had a steam engine. The steam engine made the locomotive move faster than trains pulled by horses.

The Industrial Revolution helped the growth of American cities. Before 1800, most people were farmers. Most people did not live in cities. In the 1800s more and more people began working in factories. Cities grew around these factories. As time passed, more Americans lived in cities. Fewer people lived on farms. The Industrial Revolution changed life in the United States.

Using What You've Learned

Read and Remember

Find the Answers Put a check (√) next to each sentence below that tells about the Industrial Revolution. You should check three sentences.

_____ **1** In the 1700s the British invented machines that changed how cloth was made.

_____ **2** Samuel Slater built spinning machines in the United States.

_____ **3** Cotton seeds are removed from the cotton plant after it is picked.

_____ **4** Mass production made it faster and cheaper to make goods.

Using Graphic Organizers

Cause and Effect Read each of the sentences under cause below. Then read each of the sentences under effect. Copy and complete the graphic organizer to match each cause on the left with an effect on the right.

Cause

1 It took a long time to pick seeds out of cotton, so _____

2 Francis Cabot Lowell needed workers for his cloth factories, so _____

3 More and more people began working in factories, so _____

Effect

a. he gave jobs to young women.

b. Eli Whitney invented the cotton gin.

c. cities grew around the factories.

Cause		Effect
1.	→	
2.	→	
3.	→	

Journal Writing

The Industrial Revolution changed the United States in many ways. Write a paragraph in your journal that tells about two ways the United States changed.

Skill Builder

Reading a Line Graph A **line graph** shows how something changes over time. The line graph below shows how the population of New York City changed from 1790 to 1840. The Erie Canal was finished in 1825. The Industrial Revolution and the Erie Canal helped bring many people to the city. Study the line graph.

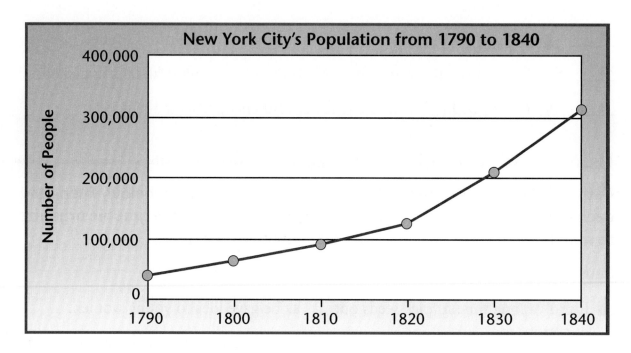

Circle the number or words that answers each question.

1 What was New York City's population in 1810?
61,000   96,000   124,000

2 In which year was the population about 203,000 people?
1800   1830   1840

3 What does the line graph show that many people began to do?
move to the city   move to farms   leave the nation

4 What happened to the population between 1790 and 1840?
stayed the same   grew slowly   grew larger

5 What was the population by 1840?
124,000   313,000   400,000

NEW WORDS

border
Trail of Tears
tariffs

PEOPLE & PLACES

North Carolina
South Carolina
Creek
South
Cherokee
Alabama
Sequoyah
Indian Territory
Oklahoma
Osceola
Seminole

Andrew Jackson

Andrew Jackson became President in 1829. He was called the "People's President."

Andrew Jackson was the seventh President of our country. He was born near the **border** between North Carolina and South Carolina in 1767. Jackson's father died before Jackson was born. In 1780 Jackson fought for America during the American Revolution. He was 13 years old. Jackson's two brothers died during the American Revolution. His mother also died during the war. Jackson had to live by himself when he was only 14 years old. After the war Jackson studied law and became a lawyer.

Andrew Jackson wanted to help his country during the War of 1812. A large group of Native Americans called the Creek lived in the South. The Creek helped the British during the War of 1812. Andrew Jackson led his soldiers against the Creek. Americans fought the Creek for many months.

Sequoyah with the Cherokee alphabet

The United States fought many battles against Native Americans. ▼

Another group of Native Americans was the Cherokee. They helped Americans fight against the Creek. In March 1814 the Creek lost an important battle in Alabama. They surrendered to Andrew Jackson and stopped fighting. The Creek had to give most of their land in Alabama and Georgia to Americans. Jackson and his soldiers also fought American Indians in Florida. Florida belonged to Spain. In 1821 Spain sold Florida to the United States for five million dollars.

Andrew Jackson became a hero. People liked him because he won the battle against the Creek and the Battle of New Orleans. Andrew Jackson became President of the United States in 1829.

Sequoyah was a Cherokee who helped Americans fight the Creek. The Cherokee spoke their own language. The Cherokee, like other groups of Native Americans, did not have an alphabet for their language.

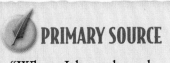
Sequoyah decided to help his people learn to read and write. He carefully studied the Cherokee language. By 1821 Sequoyah had made an alphabet for the Cherokee language. His alphabet had 85 letters.

Sequoyah helped the Cherokee learn to read and write with his alphabet. The Cherokee started the first Native American newspaper. They printed books. The Cherokee started schools. Soon almost every Cherokee could read and write Sequoyah's alphabet.

Thousands of Native Americans lived in the Southeast. Many Americans wanted to own land in the Southeast. President Jackson and these Americans believed that Native Americans should move off the land. In 1830 Congress passed a law. It said Native Americans must move to land west of the Mississippi River. They had to move to an area called Indian Territory. Today much of this land is part of the state of Oklahoma. President Jackson worked to carry out the new law.

From 1831 to 1839, many thousands of Native Americans were forced to move west to Indian Territory.

INDIAN TERRITORY, 1838

Native Americans were forced to move to Indian Territory.

G W Y   J♪Ꭷ∪Ꭴ⋅Ꭰ.

CHEROKEE   PHŒNIX.

OL. I. | **NEW ECHOTA, WEDNESDAY JUNE 4, 1828.** | **NO.**

D BY ELIAS BOUDINOTT
PRINTED WEEKLY BY
AC H. HARRIS,
R THE CHEROKEE NATION.

50 if paid in advance, $3 in six
or $3 50 if paid at the end of the

scribers who can read only the
e language the price will be $2,00
ce, or $2,50 to be paid within the

subscription will be considered as
d unless subscribers give notice to
ary before the commencement of a

erson procuring six subscribers,
ming responsible for the payment,
eive a seventh gratis.

of said river opposite to Fort Strother, on said river; all north of said line is the Cherokee lands, all south of said line is the Creek lands.

ARTICLE 2. WE THE COMMISSIONERS, do further agree that all the Creeks that are north of the said line above mentioned shall become subjects to the Cherokee nation.

ARTICLE 3. All Cherokees that are south of the said line shall become subjects of the Creek nation.

ARTICLE 4. If any chief or chiefs of the Cherokees, should fall within the Creek nation, such chief shall be continued as chief of said nation.

William Hambly,   (Seal)
    his
Big ⋈ Warrior,   (Seal)
    mark.
WITNESSES.
    Major Ridge,
    Dan'l. Griffin.
A. M'COY, Clerk N. Com.
JOS. VANN, Cl'k. to the Commissioners.

Be it remembered, This day, that I have approved of the treaty of boundary, concluded on by the Cherokees, east of the Mississippi, and the Creek nation of Indians, on the eleventh day of December, 1821, and with the modifications proposed by the committee

mitting murder on the subjects of the other, is approved and adopted; but respecting thefts, it is hereby agreed that the following rule be substituted, and adopted; viz: Should the subjects of either nation go over the line and commit theft, and he, she or they be apprehended, they shall be tried and dealt with as the laws of that nation direct, but should the person or persons so offending, make their escape and return to his, her or their nation, then, the person or persons so aggrieved, shall make application to the proper authorities of that nation for redress, and justice shall be rendered as far as practicable, agreeably to proof

⟫**Learning from Pictures** **The Cherokee started the first Native American newspaper. It was written in both English and Cherokee languages. About how old is this newspaper?**

95

Osceola

They did not want to leave their homes, farms, and villages in the Southeast. The Cherokee called the sad trip to the West the **Trail of Tears**. Many Native Americans became sick and died during the long, hard trip.

Osceola was a brave Native American who would not move west. Osceola was the leader of the Seminole in Florida. He led his people in battles against the American army. After many battles Osceola was captured. He was sent to jail. He became very sick and died. After Osceola died most of the Seminole moved west. Some Seminole stayed in Florida.

While Jackson was President, some states did not want to obey tax laws made by Congress. People in South Carolina did not want to pay **tariffs**. A tariff is a tax on goods from other countries. Tariffs make goods from other countries cost more money. The southern states bought many goods from Europe. They did not want to pay tariffs on the goods. Andrew Jackson said that all states must obey the laws of the United States. He said that he would send United States soldiers to South Carolina. South Carolina obeyed the laws. The tariffs were paid.

Andrew Jackson was President for eight years. He was called the "People's President." He believed that all people, both rich and poor, should work for their country. Jackson died in 1845.

Using Geography Themes

Movement: The Trail of Tears

The theme of **movement** tells how people, goods, and ideas move from one place to another. In the 1800s people traveled on horses, wagons, boats, or trains. Goods were sent on wagons, trains, or ships. Ideas were told by one person to another. Some ideas were shared in newspapers.

Read the paragraphs about the Trail of Tears. Study the picture below and the map on page 98.

In 1838 most Cherokee lived in Georgia and nearby states. Other Native Americans of the Southeast had been forced to move west to Indian Territory before 1838. The Cherokee were the last Native American nation to leave the Southeast.

In May 1838 the United States Army began to force about 17,000 Cherokee to leave their homes. The Cherokee were divided into groups. Some groups used land routes. They traveled through many states to reach Indian Territory. Many people walked to Indian Territory. Some rode on horses. Older people traveled in wagons. Other groups used a water route. They traveled in boats on different rivers to Indian Territory. Both routes were very dangerous.

In June 1838 the first group of Cherokee began the long trip west. The trip was more than 800 miles. The trip was hard. There was not

enough food and water. The winter was very cold. People did not have enough warm clothes and blankets. About 4,000 Cherokee died on the way to Indian Territory. The Cherokee called this hard trip the Trail of Tears. In March 1839 the last group on the Trail of Tears reached Indian Territory.

The Cherokee brought their language, religion, songs, and customs to Indian Territory. They continued to tell old Cherokee stories to their children. They started a Cherokee capital city called Tahlequah. Today more Cherokee live in Oklahoma than in any other state.

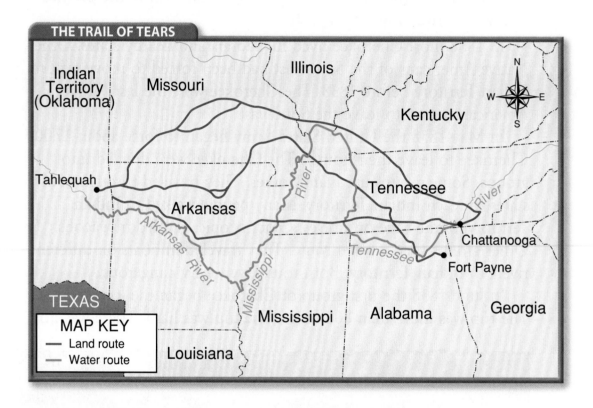

On your paper, write the answer to each question.

1. Some Cherokee rode horses along the land routes. How did other Cherokee travel on land?

2. What did Cherokee travel in if they took a water route?

3. How did children in Indian Territory learn old Cherokee stories?

4. Look at the map. What are five states the Cherokee traveled through on their land routes?

5. What were three rivers the Cherokee used on their water route?

Using What You've Learned

Read and Remember

Finish the Story Use the words in the first box to finish the first paragraph. Use the words in the second box to finish the second paragraph. Write the words you choose on the blank lines.

Paragraph 1
Creek
Spain
five
Florida
Territory
Trail of Tears
tariff

Paragraph 2
newspaper
west
Florida
Army
Osceola
alphabet
Cherokee

During the War of 1812, Andrew Jackson fought against a group of Native Americans called the **(1)** _____ . Jackson also fought against Native Americans in **(2)** _____ . In 1821 **(3)** _____ sold Florida to the United States for **(4)** _____ million dollars. As President, Jackson said all states must obey the **(5)** _____ laws. Jackson also forced Native Americans to move west to Indian **(6)** _____ . Many Native Americans became sick and died as they moved west. The Cherokee called the sad trip to the West the **(7)** _____ .

Two famous Native Americans lived during the time of Andrew Jackson. Sequoyah was a **(8)** _____ . He helped his people by making the first Native American **(9)** _____ . It had 85 letters. The Cherokee used it to print books and a **(10)** _____ . The famous leader of the Seminole in Florida was **(11)** _____ . This brave leader would not move **(12)** _____ . He fought many battles against the United States **(13)** _____ . After Osceola died, most Native Americans in **(14)** _____ were forced to move west.

Think and Apply

Fact or Opinion Read each sentence below. Write an **F** next to each sentence that tells a fact. Write an **O** next to each sentence that tells an opinion. You should find six opinions.

_____ **1)** Andrew Jackson fought the Creek.

_____ **2)** The United States paid too much money to Spain for Florida.

_____ **3)** Sequoyah was a Cherokee.

_____ **4)** Sequoyah spent too much time making the alphabet.

_____ **5)** The Cherokee made the first Native American newspaper.

_____ **6)** The Cherokee newspaper had many interesting stories.

_____ **7)** Jackson believed that Native Americans should move west of the Mississippi River.

_____ **8)** The Cherokee moved to Indian Territory.

_____ **9)** Many Native Americans died during the long, hard trip to Indian Territory.

_____ **10)** Osceola wanted to stay in Florida.

_____ **11)** The United States Congress can write tax laws.

_____ **12)** States should not have to pay tariffs.

_____ **13)** Andrew Jackson was a better President than Thomas Jefferson.

_____ **14)** Andrew Jackson was a good President.

Journal Writing

Imagine that you and your family are Native Americans. You are forced to move west. Think about how you would feel. In your journal, write four or five sentences telling about your feelings. Be sure to tell why you feel the way you do.

Americans Work for Reform

NEW WORDS

reform
education
abolitionists
mental illness

PEOPLE & PLACES

Horace Mann
Emma Willard
Mary Lyon
Mount Holyoke
   Female Seminary
Oberlin College
Ohio
Thomas Gallaudet
Connecticut
William Lloyd
   Garrison
Frederick Douglass
North
Dorothea Dix
Elizabeth Cady
   Stanton
Seneca Falls

Frederick Douglass worked to end slavery.

Should there be free schools for all children? Should there be laws to end slavery? Should men and women have the same rights? People asked these questions in the early 1800s. Many people answered "no" to these questions. Other people wanted to improve the country. These Americans began to work for **reform**.

In the early 1800s, there were no laws that said children must go to school. Many children worked on farms and in factories. Children from rich families went to fine private schools. But children from poor families did not attend good schools. They often went to public schools that had only one big classroom. All grades were in the classroom. These schools had only one teacher. There were few books. There were not very many high schools.

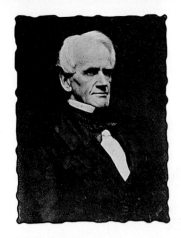

Horace Mann

Mary Lyon

Horace Mann worked to improve public schools in Massachusetts. He worked to have the state pay for children to go to public schools. People built bigger schools that had many classrooms. People built more high schools. Mann started the first school to teach people how to be good teachers. He also helped teachers earn higher pay.

Massachusetts had better schools because of Horace Mann. Other states began to improve their schools, too. States passed laws that said children must go to school.

At that time girls could not get the same **education** that boys could. Often they could only go to school if there was room. This was usually in the summer. Girls were not taught science or math. Girls were not allowed to go to college.

Emma Willard helped girls get a better education. She started the first high school for girls.

Mary Lyon also helped women get a better education. She decided to start a college for women. It was called Mount Holyoke Female Seminary. Mount Holyoke opened in Massachusetts in 1837. Women at Mount Holyoke studied the same subjects that men studied in other colleges.

Soon other colleges for women were started. Women were allowed to study in some colleges with men. Oberlin College in Ohio became the first college for men and women. It also had many African American students.

Mary Lyon began Mount Holyoke Female Seminary. It later became Mount Holyoke College.

At first there were few schools for children with special needs. Thomas Gallaudet believed deaf children should go to school. In 1817 he started a free school for deaf children in Connecticut.

In the 1830s, there were more than two million African American slaves in the United States. Most of them lived in the South. Some Americans believed slavery was wrong. They wanted all slaves to be free. The people who worked to end slavery were called **abolitionists**. William Lloyd Garrison became an abolitionist leader. He published a newspaper about ending slavery.

Frederick Douglass was an African American abolitionist. Douglass had been a slave. He ran away to the North and became free. Douglass gave many speeches. Again and again he told people why slavery was wrong. Many people heard Frederick Douglass and became abolitionists.

Dorothea Dix was another American who worked for reform. Dix visited many jails. She worked to make jails better for prisoners. Dix also saw that many prisoners were in jails because they had **mental illness**. She said these people should not be in jail. Dix said people with mental illness should be treated in hospitals. She helped start hospitals to care for people with mental illness.

Dorothea Dix

Learning from Pictures William Lloyd Garrison published this newspaper about ending slavery. Where was this newspaper published?

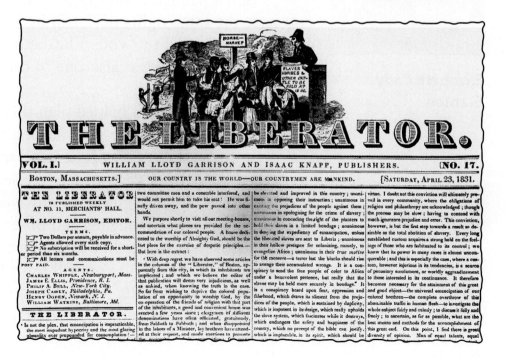

Elizabeth Cady Stanton spoke about women's rights at a meeting in Seneca Falls in 1848.

Elizabeth Cady Stanton

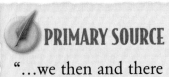
In the 1800s the fight for women's rights began. Some people felt that women were not treated fairly. Women were not allowed to vote. Married women had to give their money to their husbands. Women could not get good jobs. They could not become doctors or lawyers. Women who worked earned much less money than men did.

Some women abolitionists decided that women should have the same rights that men had. They wanted women to have the right to vote. Elizabeth Cady Stanton was an abolitionist. She was also one of the leaders in the fight for women's rights.

In 1848 Stanton helped plan the first large meeting about women's rights. The meeting was in Seneca Falls, New York. About 240 women and men came to the meeting. Stanton gave a speech. She said women should be allowed to vote. She told why women needed more rights. Frederick Douglass and other people joined the fight for women's rights. Slowly, women did win more rights. In Chapter 32 you will learn how women won the right to vote in 1920.

Many people in the United States worked for reform in the 1800s. They wanted Americans to have better lives.

Using What You've Learned

Read and Remember

Match Up Finish each sentence in Group A with words from Group B. Write the letter of the correct answer on the blank line.

Group A

1 In the early 1800s, there were not enough good _____ .

2 Thomas Gallaudet started a free school for _____ .

3 Women could not become doctors or _____ .

4 Elizabeth Cady Stanton said women should be allowed _____ .

Group B

a. to vote

b. deaf children

c. public schools

d. lawyers

Think and Apply

Finding the Main Idea Read each group of sentences below. One of the sentences is a main idea. Two sentences support the main idea. Write an M next to the sentence that is the main idea in each group.

1 _____ There were problems in American education in the 1800s.
_____ There were no laws that said children must go to school.
_____ There were few schools for children with disabilities.

2 _____ Girls were not taught science and math.
_____ Only boys were allowed to go to college.
_____ Girls did not get the same education that boys did.

3 _____ Emma Willard started the first high school for girls.
_____ People tried to help girls get a better education.
_____ Mary Lyon started Mount Holyoke Female Seminary.

4 _____ William Lloyd Garrison began a newspaper about ending slavery.
_____ Frederick Douglass spoke about why slavery was wrong.
_____ Some Americans wanted to end slavery.

Skill Builder

Reading a Chart A **chart** lists a group of facts. Charts help you learn facts quickly. Read the chart below to learn how some Americans worked for reform in the 1800s.

Americans Who Worked for Reform in the 1800s		
Name	**Place**	**Important Work**
Horace Mann	Massachusetts	Mann improved education in public schools in Massachusetts.
Mary Lyon	Massachusetts	Lyon started Mount Holyoke Female Seminary for women.
Thomas Gallaudet	Connecticut	Gallaudet started the first school for deaf children in the United States.
Frederick Douglass	New York and other states	Douglass was an abolitionist. He worked to end slavery.
Dorothea Dix	Massachusetts	Dix helped start hospitals to treat people with mental illness.
Elizabeth Cady Stanton	New York	Stanton worked for women's rights.

Draw a circle around the words that finish each sentence.

1. To read the names of people who worked for reform, read the chart from _____ .
   left to right   top to bottom   the middle

2. To learn all about Mary Lyon, read the chart from _____ .
   left to right   top to bottom   bottom to top

3. The person who improved public schools in Massachusetts was _____ .
   Thomas Gallaudet   Horace Mann   Dorothea Dix

4. The person who was an abolitionist was _____ .
   Mary Lyon   Dorothea Dix   Frederick Douglass

5. Elizabeth Cady Stanton worked for _____ .
   women's rights   better schools   hospitals for mental illnesses

Review

Study the time line on this page. Then use the words and date in blue print to finish the story. Write the words and date you choose on the correct blank lines.

cities	Louisiana	reform
1812	women's rights	doubled
Cherokee	Industrial Revolution	factory

Many changes took place in the United States as it grew. The United States **(1)** _____ its size when it bought **(2)** _____ from France in 1803. The United States showed it was strong when it fought a second war against Great Britain from **(3)** _____ to 1814. Many Americans wanted to own Native American land. Native Americans were forced to move west. The **(4)** _____ were forced to move to Indian Territory in 1838.

The **(5)** _____ began in the United States in 1790 when Samuel Slater built a **(6)** _____ for spinning thread. During the 1800s fewer people lived on farms. More Americans moved to **(7)** _____ . People built steamboats, canals, and railroads to help move goods. Many people worked for **(8)** _____ in the United States. Elizabeth Cady Stanton gave a speech about **(9)** _____ in Seneca Falls in 1848.

Samuel Slater builds a factory for spinning thread.
1790

The United States buys Louisiana and New Orleans from France.
1803

The War of 1812 begins.
1812

Sequoyah invents the Cherokee alphabet.
1821

The Cherokee are forced to move to Indian Territory.
1838

| 1790 | 1800 | 1810 | 1820 | 1830 | 1840 | 1850 |

1793
Eli Whitney invents the cotton gin.

1814
Andrew Jackson's army wins a battle against the Creek.

1825
The Erie Canal is finished.

1848
A women's rights meeting is held in Seneca Falls.

The Nation Grows and Divides

Stephen F. Austin starts an American colony in Texas.
1821

1820   1830

Suppose you are living in the United States in 1860. Everyone believes there will be a war between the northern states and the southern states. You must choose a side to fight for in this war. You might have to fight against your own family during the war. You might have to fight against your best friend. Thousands will die during the Civil War.

The years between 1821 and 1865 were years of great change. Many Americans moved west. Areas in the West became new states. The problem of slavery also grew. The northern states did not like slavery. The southern states said they needed slaves. In 1861 the terrible Civil War began.

Read to Learn

- What would you have done if you had lived between 1821 and 1865?

- Would you have moved west?

- Would you have fought for the northern states or for the southern states?

Texas wins independence from Mexico.
1836

Texas becomes a state.
1845

The United States wins the Mexican War.
1848

Abraham Lincoln becomes President. The Civil War begins.
1861

1840

1850

1860

1870

1843
People go to Oregon on the Oregon Trail.

1846
A treaty is signed about Oregon.

1850
California becomes a state.

1859
Oregon becomes a state.

1865
The Civil War ends.

Independence for Texas

➤ **Learning from Pictures How did Americans and Mexicans travel to Texas in the 1820s?**

Mexico belonged to Spain for 300 years. In 1821 Mexico became an independent country. At that time, Texas was part of Mexico.

Moses Austin wanted to start a colony for Americans in Texas. He died before he could start the colony. His son, Stephen F. Austin, decided to continue his father's plan to settle Texas. Few Mexicans lived in Texas. So the leaders of Mexico wanted Americans to move to Texas.

Stephen F. Austin started an American colony in Texas in 1821. The land was good for growing cotton and for raising cattle. African Americans, German Americans, and Asian Americans moved to Texas. Jewish Americans and many people from Europe also settled in Texas. More people from Mexico went to

Stephen F. Austin

live in Texas. By 1830 there were many more Americans than Mexicans in Texas. People who live in Texas are called Texans.

Many Mexicans were angry that Americans brought slaves to Texas. Mexican law did not allow slavery in Texas. Mexicans wanted the Americans to obey this law. The Americans did not listen.

Mexico's leaders were worried that Texas might want to become part of the United States. In 1830 Mexico made a new law. The law said that Americans could no longer come to live in Texas. Americans in Texas did not like this law.

Texans did not like other Mexican laws. They did not like the law that said Texans must speak Spanish. Another Mexican law said settlers must be Catholic. Texans wanted to help write laws for Texas. Mexico would not let the settlers make laws for Texas.

The Mexican government became angry with the new settlers. The government was angry that slaves were brought to Texas. Few Texans spoke Spanish. Many Texans were not Catholic.

▲ **Stephen F. Austin sold land to many families who wanted to move to Texas.**

Antonio López de Santa Anna

Suzanna Dickenson

José Antonio Navarro

Santa Anna and his soldiers attacked the Texans at the Alamo. ▶

Mexican soldiers went to Texas to force the Texans to obey Mexican laws. This made the Texans angry. Some Texans began to fight the Mexican soldiers.

Antonio López de Santa Anna was the Mexican president. He led his army against the Texans. In 1836 there were about 180 Texan soldiers in a mission called the Alamo. The Texans used the Alamo as a **fort**. Santa Anna and about 4,000 Mexican soldiers attacked the Alamo. The Texans were very brave. They fought for 13 days. Santa Anna won the Battle of the Alamo. His army killed every Texan soldier.

Some of the Texan soldiers had brought their wives and children to the Alamo. One of these wives was Suzanna Dickenson. After the battle, Santa Anna sent her to tell other Texans not to fight against Mexico.

Texan leaders met in March 1836 while the soldiers were fighting at the Alamo. The leaders wrote a declaration of independence for Texas. This declaration said that Texas was no longer part of Mexico.

Some Mexican Texans also wanted an independent Texas. José Antonio Navarro was a Mexican who was born

Santa Anna surrendered to Sam Houston after the battle at the San Jacinto River. ▷

Lorenzo de Zavala

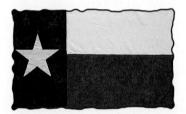

Texas flag

THE REPUBLIC OF TEXAS

UNITED STATES

REPUBLIC OF TEXAS

Alamo

San Jacinto

MEXICO

KEY
✳ Battle site

Important battles

in Texas. He was a friend of Stephen F. Austin. He signed the Texas Declaration of Independence. He later helped write a new constitution for Texas. Lorenzo de Zavala was born in Mexico. He came to live in Texas with his family. De Zavala also signed the Texas Declaration of Independence. He told all Texans to fight for freedom.

Sam Houston became the general of the Texas army. He learned about the Battle of the Alamo from Suzanna Dickenson. Houston told his soldiers to remember the brave people who died at the Alamo.

On April 21, 1836, Sam Houston led the Texans against Santa Anna's army. They fought at the San Jacinto River. "Remember the Alamo!" Houston's soldiers shouted as they fought the Mexican soldiers. The battle lasted only 18 minutes. The Texans won. Antonio López de Santa Anna surrendered to Sam Houston. Texas was now free. The Texans called their war against Mexico the **Texas Revolution**.

Texas was no longer part of Mexico, and Texas was not part of the United States. Texas became a **republic**. A republic is an independent country. Sam Houston became the first president of the Republic of Texas. Lorenzo de Zavala became the vice president.

Texans wanted Texas to become part of the United States. But they would have to wait almost ten more years before Texas became a state.

113

Using Primary Sources

Letters from William Barrett Travis

William Barrett Travis led the Texan soldiers at the Battle of the Alamo. On March 6, 1836, Santa Anna and his large army captured the Alamo. They killed Travis and the other Texan soldiers. During Travis's last days at the Alamo, he wrote letters asking Americans and Texans to help. Here are parts of three of his letters.

promptly
soon

provisions
food

victory
a win

relief
help

peril
put in danger

> *February 23, 1836*
> *We have removed all our men into the Alamo. . . . We hope you will send us all the men you can spare **promptly**. . . . We have but little **provisions**. . . .*
>
> *February 24, 1836*
> *. . . The enemy has demanded a surrender. . . . I shall never surrender. . . . I call on you . . . to come to our aid. . . . **Victory** or Death. . . .*
>
> *March 3, 1836*
> *I am still here. . . . I have held this place 10 days against . . . 1,500 to 6,000, and shall continue to hold it till I get **relief** from my countrymen. . . .*
>
> *Make a declaration of independence, and we will then understand, and the world will understand, what we are fighting for. . . . Under the flag of independence, we are ready to **peril** our lives. . . .*

On your paper, write the answer to each question.

1. Where were Travis and his men on February 23, 1836?

2. On February 23 what did Travis say he hoped Texans would do?

3. What did the enemy want Travis to do on February 24?

4. How many days had Travis been inside the Alamo as of March 3?

5. **Think and Write** Travis and the Texan soldiers would not surrender at the Alamo. They were willing to fight for "Victory or Death." Why do you think they would do this?

Using What You've Learned

Read and Remember

Choose a Word Choose the best word or words in blue print to finish each sentence. Write the word or words you choose on the correct blank.

Sam Houston	**Santa Anna**	**Texas Revolution**
Alamo	**de Zavala**	**Stephen F. Austin**

1 _____ started an American colony in Texas.

2 The leader of the Mexican army was President _____ .

3 About 180 Texan soldiers died at the _____ .

4 José Antonio Navarro and Lorenzo _____ were Mexican Texans who signed the Texas Declaration of Independence.

5 The leader of the Texas army and the first president of the Republic of Texas was _____ .

6 The war for Texan independence was called the _____ .

Think and Apply

Understanding Different Points of View Mexicans and Texans had different points of view about Texas. Read the sentences below. Write **Texan** next to the sentences that show the Texan point of view. Write **Mexican** next to the sentences that show the Mexican point of view.

_____ **1** People in Texas should obey Mexican laws.

_____ **2** People in Texas should write their own laws.

_____ **3** Everyone in Texas must be Catholic.

_____ **4** Americans in Texas do not have to be Catholic.

_____ **5** Americans can bring slaves to Texas.

_____ **6** Americans cannot have slaves in Texas.

_____ **7** Americans should speak Spanish in Texas.

_____ **8** Americans can speak English in Texas.

NEW WORDS

Manifest Destiny
citizens
Mexican Cession
Gadsden Purchase
property

PEOPLE & PLACES

James K. Polk
Rio Grande
Mexico City
Nevada
Utah
Arizona
Colorado
Mexican Americans

The United States Grows Larger

When the flag of the Republic of Texas was lowered, Texas became the twenty-eighth state in the United States.

In Chapter 17 you read that Texans won their war against Mexico and started a republic. Santa Anna had surrendered to the Texans. But Mexican leaders did not accept his surrender. The Mexicans said that Texas was still part of Mexico. Texans wanted Texas to become part of the United States. The Mexicans said there would be a war if Texas became part of the United States.

Many Americans wanted Texas to become a state. They believed in an idea called **Manifest Destiny**. Manifest Destiny meant the United States should rule land from the Atlantic Ocean to the Pacific Ocean. This idea also meant that the United States should become a larger and stronger country.

James K. Polk

LAND CLAIMED BY MEXICO

UNITED STATES

Texas land claimed by Mexico

Texas

Rio Grande

MEXICO

The United States and Mexico fought a war over Texas land.

James K. Polk became President in 1845. The new President believed in Manifest Destiny. He wanted Texas to become a state. He also tried to buy California and New Mexico from Mexico. But Mexico refused to sell its land.

In 1845 the United States Congress voted for Texas to become a state. This made the Mexican government very angry.

In 1846 a war started between the United States and Mexico. The two countries did not agree on the border for Texas. The United States said a river called the Rio Grande was the southern border for Texas. Mexico said the size of Texas should be smaller. The Mexicans said that much of the land north of the Rio Grande belonged to Mexico.

The United States and Mexico sent soldiers to the Rio Grande. The soldiers began to fight. This war was called the Mexican War. During the war American soldiers captured California and New Mexico. The Mexican soldiers were brave. They did not stop fighting. Americans and Mexicans continued to fight. In 1847 American soldiers went into Mexico. They captured Mexico City, the capital of Mexico. Soon the Mexicans surrendered. The war was over.

American soldiers stand in Mexico City after capturing this capital city of Mexico.

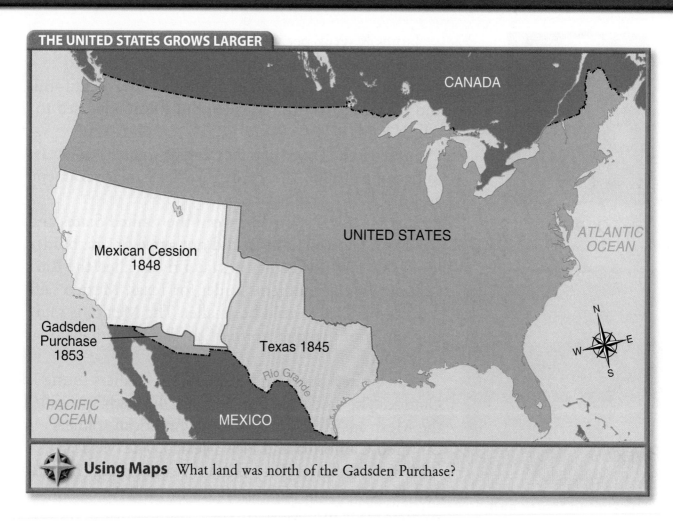

Using Maps What land was north of the Gadsden Purchase?

The leaders of the United States and Mexico signed a peace treaty in 1848. The treaty gave the United States a large area of Mexican land. It also said that Texas belonged to the United States. The Rio Grande became the border between Texas and Mexico. The treaty also said that Mexicans in the Southwest could become American **citizens**. The United States gave Mexico $15 million for land taken during the war.

The land that the United States got in 1848 was called the **Mexican Cession**. Find the Mexican Cession on the map above. The land from the Mexican Cession became California, Nevada, Utah, Arizona, and parts of New Mexico and Colorado. The United States now owned land from the Atlantic Ocean to the Pacific Ocean.

Americans wanted a railroad across the southern part of the United States. In 1853 the United States gave Mexico $10 million for the land in the **Gadsden Purchase**. Find the Gadsden Purchase on the map above. Years later, Americans built a railroad across the Gadsden Purchase.

Mexicans in the Southwest became American citizens after the Mexican War. They were called Mexican Americans.

Mexican Americans helped their new country. They taught Americans how to grow food on land where there was little rain. Mexican Americans helped build railroads for the United States. They helped other Americans look for gold and silver in the Southwest. They taught Americans how to be cowboys.

Mexican Americans helped the United States change a law that was unfair to women. Before the Mexican War, a married American woman could not own **property**. Her husband owned everything. Mexican law was fairer to women. Mexican women owned property together with their husbands. After the Mexican War, Americans changed their law so that women could own property with their husbands.

The land of the United States went from the Atlantic Ocean to the Pacific Ocean. The United States had become a strong country with a lot of new land and many new people.

Learning from Pictures Mexican Americans in the Southwest taught Americans many things, including how to be cowboys. What kind of clothing did a cowboy wear?

Using What You've Learned

Read and Remember

Choose the Answer Draw a circle around the correct answer.

1. Which President believed in Manifest Destiny?
   James Madison   Andrew Jackson   James K. Polk

2. When did Texas become a state?
   1776   1845   1900

3. What city did American soldiers capture during the Mexican War?
   Boston   Washington, D.C.   Mexico City

4. Which river became the border for Texas?
   Mississippi River   St. Lawrence River   Rio Grande

5. How much did the United States pay for the Mexican Cession?
   $5 million $15 million $30 million

6. Which three states were among those made from the Mexican Cession?
   California, Nevada, Arizona   New York, New Jersey, Florida
   Texas, Mississippi, Oklahoma

7. What land did the United States buy in 1853?
   Louisiana Purchase   Gadsden Purchase   Florida

8. Why did the United States want the Gadsden Purchase?
   for its water   for a railroad   for a park

Skill Builder

Reviewing Map Directions Look back at the map on page 118. Draw a circle around the word that finishes each sentence.

1. The Gadsden Purchase is _____ of Mexico.
   east   south   north

2. The Pacific Ocean is _____ of the Mexican Cession.
   southeast   east   west

3. The Rio Grande is _____ of the Gadsden Purchase.
   northwest   southwest   east

4 Mexico is _____ of the United States.

south   north   west

5 Texas is _____ of the Gadsden Purchase.

east   southwest   west

Using Graphic Organizers

Cause and Effect Read each of the sentences under cause below. Then read each of the sentences under effect. Copy and complete the graphic organizer to match each cause on the left with an effect on the right.

Cause

1 In 1845 many Americans believed their country should be larger, so _____

2 Texas became a state, so _____

3 In 1848 the United States got land in the Mexican Cession, so _____

4 Americans wanted to build a railroad across the southern part of the United States, so _____

Effect

a. they paid Mexico $10 million for land in the Gadsden Purchase.

b. Mexico said there would be a war with the United States.

c. the country's borders went from the Atlantic Ocean to the Pacific Ocean.

d. the United States Congress voted for Texas to become a state.

Cause		Effect
1.	→	
2.	→	
3.	→	
4.	→	

Journal Writing

Mexicans who lived in the Southwest became American citizens after the Mexican War. Write a paragraph in your journal that tells how Mexican Americans helped the United States.

On to Oregon and California

⮞ **Learning from Pictures In what ways was the trip over the Rocky Mountains to Oregon hard?**

Many Americans wanted to move west to Oregon Country in the 1840s. Oregon had lots of trees for building new houses. Oregon had good land for farming. Soon thousands of Americans moved west to build new homes and farms in Oregon Country.

The trip to Oregon Country was long and slow. There were no roads across the United States to Oregon. Families traveled to Oregon in covered wagons. Horses and **oxen** pulled the covered wagons. In 1843 many families in 120 covered wagons met in Independence, Missouri. These 120 covered wagons made a **wagon train**. The covered wagons traveled together across the Great Plains and the Rocky Mountains to Oregon. The trail they followed became known as the **Oregon Trail**.

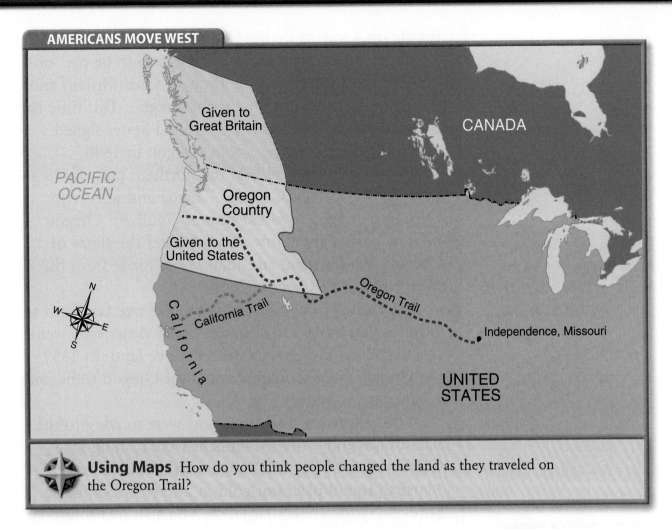

Given to
Great Britain

CANADA

PACIFIC
OCEAN

Oregon
Country

Given to the
United States

Oregon Trail

California Trail

California

Independence, Missouri

UNITED
STATES

N
W E
S

 **Using Maps** How do you think people changed the land as they traveled on the Oregon Trail?

What was it like to travel on the Oregon Trail? Families woke up very early every day. Then people traveled as many hours as they could. At night they slept on the floors of their covered wagons. When it rained, wagon wheels got stuck in mud. Sometimes wagons turned over. Then people inside the wagons were hurt or killed. It was hard to find food on the way to Oregon. Many families were hungry. The wagons traveled across mountains, forests, and rivers. The long trip on the Oregon Trail took about six months.

At last the families reached Oregon Country. They had traveled nearly 2,000 miles. Soon thousands of other people went to Oregon on the Oregon Trail. Each year more people settled along the Pacific **coast**.

Oregon Country was much bigger than our state of Oregon today. Oregon Country included part of Canada. Great Britain and the United States had shared Oregon Country for many years. The two nations could not

PRIMARY SOURCE

"The way looks pleasant . . . we are so near . . . the difficulties of an unheard-of journey for females."

–Narcissa Whitman

123

decide on a way to divide Oregon. President Polk believed in Manifest Destiny. He wanted Oregon to be part of the United States. Many people thought Great Britain and the United States would fight for Oregon. This time the two nations did not fight. The United States signed a treaty with Great Britain about Oregon in 1846.

The 1846 treaty said that the northern part of Oregon Country was part of Canada. Canada and northern Oregon belonged to Great Britain. Southern Oregon became part of the United States. Later the states of Oregon, Washington, and Idaho were made from the southern part of Oregon Country.

The United States government gave free farmland to families that moved to Oregon. Many Americans went to Oregon on the Oregon Trail for free land. In 1859 the United States Congress voted for Oregon to become a state.

While thousands of Americans were moving to the state of Oregon, other Americans were rushing to California. One day in 1848, a man named James Marshall found pieces of gold in a river in California. Soon everyone knew that James Marshall had found gold.

People from all over the United States began moving to California. They wanted to find gold and become rich.

Many people moved to California to look for gold. ▽

James Beckwourth found a mountain pass that made it easier for Americans to travel west. ▶

We say that California had a **gold rush** in 1848 and 1849 because thousands of people went to find gold.

The gold rush brought many kinds of people to California. Many people came from Europe to look for gold in California. People came from China to find gold. Free African Americans also moved to California.

James Beckwourth made it easier for many people to travel west to California. Beckwourth was an African American. He moved west and lived with Native Americans. Tall mountains in the West made it hard to go to California. Beckwourth looked for an easier way to go across the mountains. At last Beckwourth found a **pass** through the mountains. Many people used this pass to reach California. Today that pass through the mountains is called the Beckwourth Pass.

Some people were lucky in California. They found gold and became rich. Most people did not find gold. Many people stayed in California. They built farms and factories. They started new cities. They built stores and houses. By 1850, 90,000 people were living in California. The United States Congress voted for California to become a state in 1850.

The California gold rush brought thousands of settlers to California. The Oregon Trail brought thousands of Americans to the Northwest. Every year more Americans moved west to California and Oregon.

Using Geography Themes

Human/Environment Interaction: The Gold Rush

The theme of **human/environment interaction** tells how people live in an area. People in cold areas wear coats. People near oceans might fish for their food. The theme also tells how people can change an area. People use the land to help them live and work. They cut down trees to build houses and roads. They build canals so that ships can reach rivers or lakes.

Read the paragraphs about California's gold rush. Study the photo below and the map on page 127.

Beginning in 1848, thousands of people rushed to California to search for gold. They started many mining camps. This gold rush changed California's land and rivers. The **environment** also changed how the **miners** lived.

When the gold rush began, people used their hands and tools to remove gold from rivers. Soon the gold in these rivers was gone. After 1850, miners began digging deep in the earth to find gold. Some miners built strong walls called **dams** to hold back the water in rivers. Then they dug deep into the ground where there had been water. Many miners dug tunnels to find gold. Others used huge amounts of water to break open mountain walls to find gold.

As the miners dug into the earth, dirt and rocks were dumped into rivers. The rivers became dirty. Most of the fish in the dirty rivers died.

The environment changed the lives of the miners. Miners spent most of their days searching for gold. At night, they often slept in tents on cold ground. When the fish died in the dirty rivers, miners had less food to eat. Sometimes the rivers spread lots of rocks over farmland. Farmers could not grow enough fruits and vegetables for miners to eat. Many miners became very sick because they did not eat well or sleep well.

Sutter Creek, California, was a mining town that began in 1848. The miners lived in tents. The town grew as more gold was found. The miners built houses. Today the gold is gone. Many people in Sutter Creek now sell wood from nearby forests to earn money.

MINING CAMPS OF CALIFORNIA'S GOLD RUSH

MAP KEY
★ Capital City
● City
Mining camp
Mountains
----- Present-day border

Nevada

California

Sacramento ★

Sutter Creek

San Francisco

PACIFIC OCEAN

On your paper, write the answer to each question.

1. Where did people look for gold at the start of California's gold rush?
2. What are three things the miners did to the earth in order to find gold?
3. Why did the fish die in many of California's rivers?
4. How did the lives of miners change when many fish were gone?
5. Why couldn't farmers grow enough crops for miners to eat?
6. How do many people in Sutter Creek earn money today?

127

Using What You've Learned

Read and Remember

Finish the Sentence Draw a circle around the date, word, or words that finish each sentence.

1. Thousands of Americans went to Oregon Country in the _____ .
   1820s   1830s   1840s

2. The Oregon Trail began in _____ .
   Philadelphia   New Orleans   Independence

3. In 1846 the northern part of Oregon Country became part of _____ .
   the United States   Canada   Washington

4. Families that moved to Oregon were given free _____ .
   wagons   houses   farmland

5. California's gold rush began when _____ found gold in a river.
   James Marshall   James Beckwourth   President Polk

6. In 1848 and 1849, Americans rushed to California to find _____ .
   silver   gold   trees

Think and Apply

Categories Read the words in each group. Decide how they are alike. Find the best title in blue print for each group. Write the title on the line above each group.

James Beckwourth
California

Oregon Trail
Gold Rush

1. _____
   1848 and 1849
   search for gold
   brought thousands to California

2. _____
   African American
   lived in the West
   found a pass through the mountains

3. _____
   horses and oxen
   covered wagons
   went to Oregon

4. _____
   gold rush
   new cities
   90,000 people in 1850

Skill Builder

Reading a Historical Map The map below shows how the United States became a large country. Study each area and when it became part of the United States.

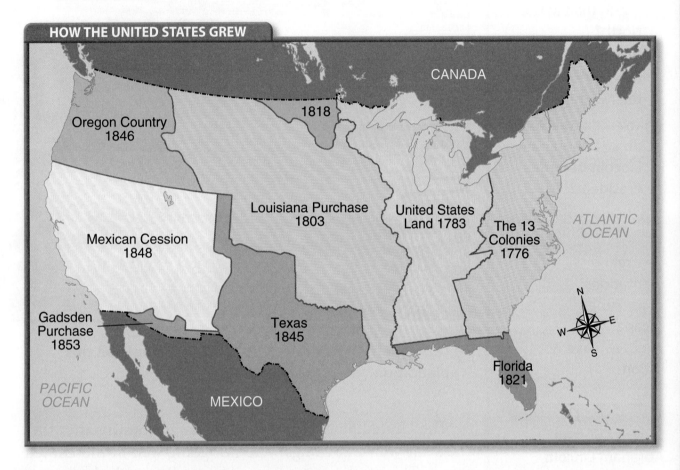

HOW THE UNITED STATES GREW

Draw a circle around the correct answer.

① What land made up the United States in 1776?

Texas   the 13 Colonies   Louisiana

② What southeast land belonged to Spain until 1821?

Oregon Country   Texas   Florida

③ Which northwest land became part of the United States in 1846?

Oregon Country   Florida   Louisiana Purchase

④ What land did the United States get in 1848?

Mexican Cession   Louisiana Purchase   Texas

⑤ Which land did the United States buy in 1853?

Gadsden Purchase   Oregon Country   Texas

The Southern States Leave

▶ **Learning from Pictures** Who are these people on this plantation? What are they doing?

The United States had become a large country after the Mexican War. But things were not going well in the United States. The northern states were **quarreling** with the southern states. The northern states were called the North, and the southern states were called the South. Why did the North and South quarrel?

An important problem was slavery. In the early days of our nation, there were slaves both in the North and in the South. But farms were small in the North. The North had many factories. Most people there did not need slaves on their farms and in factories. There were fewer slaves in the North.

In the South some people owned very large farms called **plantations**. The owners grew cotton, **sugar cane**, and tobacco on their plantations. Plantation owners needed many workers. Many plantation owners bought slaves to do the work. The plantation owners thought they could not grow crops without slaves.

A small group of rich plantation owners owned most of the slaves. Most people in the South did not own any slaves. But almost everyone in the South agreed that slavery should be allowed. The North did not agree.

After the Mexican War, more Americans moved to the West. People from the South started new plantations in the West. They wanted to bring their slaves. The northern states did not want slavery in the West.

The North and South began to quarrel. In the North many people said that all people should be free. They said that it was not right for one person to own another person. In the South people said that the Constitution allowed slavery. People in the South said that people in the North should not tell them what to do. The people in the North wanted to make new laws against slavery in the West. This made the South very angry.

Plantation owners in the South bought and sold slaves. ▼

Abolitionists helped many slaves escape to the North.

Harriet Tubman

The South was worried because many Americans had become abolitionists. They were working to end slavery. Some abolitionists wrote books and newspapers that told why slavery was wrong. Some people gave speeches against slavery. Other people helped slaves run away from their owners.

Harriet Tubman was one of the people who helped slaves become free. She had been a slave herself. She had run away to the North. In the North she was free. Tubman went back to the South and helped slaves **escape** to Canada. In Canada they were free. Harriet Tubman helped many people get their freedom.

In 1850 Congress passed a law about slaves who escaped to the North. It was called the **Fugitive Slave Act**. The new law said that slaves who ran away must be returned to the South. People who did not return them were punished. This new law made the North very angry with the South.

In 1861 a man named Abraham Lincoln became the President of the United States. What kind of man was Abraham Lincoln? He came from a poor family. He lived very far from school when he was young. He only went to school for about one year. Lincoln learned as much as he could by reading books. He grew up to be very tall, thin,

Abraham Lincoln came from a poor family. ▶

Abraham Lincoln

Jefferson Davis

and strong. He became a lawyer. Many people liked Lincoln because he was honest and smart.

President Lincoln believed that slavery was wrong. He promised he would not try to end slavery in the South. But he said slavery should not be allowed in the West. The North liked what Lincoln said, but the South did not. The South believed Lincoln would work to end slavery everywhere.

Seven southern states decided they no longer wanted to be part of the **Union**. The Union is another name for the United States. In 1861 these seven southern states started a new country. They called their country the Confederate States of America. The Confederate States wrote their own constitution. It had laws that allowed slavery. The Confederate States had their own flag and their own money. Jefferson Davis became the president of the Confederate States. Soon four other southern states joined the Confederate States.

President Lincoln said that the United States must be one country, not two. Would the Union and the Confederate States become one country again? Would it take a war to bring them together? Read Chapter 21 to find the answers to these questions.

Using Geography Themes

Region: The South in 1861

The theme of **region** tells how places in an area are alike. A region can be large or small. Places in a region might have the same weather or kind of land. People in a region might share customs, ideas, and ways of life.

Read the paragraphs about the South in 1861. Study the picture below and the map on page 135.

The South was a region with huge plantations. Plantations were the center of southern life. The South was a good place for farms and plantations. There was plenty of good soil. There were rain and a warm **climate** during most of the year. Plantation owners grew crops such as cotton, sugar cane, tobacco, and rice. Cotton was the most important crop. The South earned most of its money by selling its cotton.

Slaves did most of the farm work on the plantations. Plantation owners believed they could not grow cotton and other crops without the work of slaves. By 1861 one third of the people in the South were African American slaves.

The South was very different from the North. It did not have many big cities, factories, and railroads like the North. New Orleans was the biggest city in the South. But it was smaller than many cities in the North.

While many people in the North were moving to cities, most people in the South worked at farming. Many people owned small farms. Most of the farmers did not own slaves. But almost everyone in the South agreed that the region needed slavery.

In 1861 most people in the South said they would fight to keep their slaves and their way of life. Seven southern states decided to leave the United States. They did not want to be part of a country that might end slavery. They started a new country called the Confederate States of America. Later four other states joined the Confederate States.

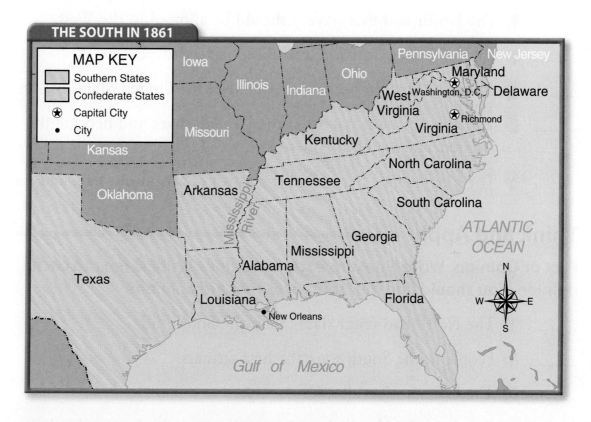

THE SOUTH IN 1861

MAP KEY
Southern States
Confederate States
★ Capital City
• City

On your paper, write the answer to each question.

1. Why was the South a good place for farms and plantations?
2. What was the most important crop in the South?
3. How was the South different from the North?
4. Why did some southern states start a new country?
5. Look at the map. Which four southern states did **not** join the Confederate States of America?

135

Using What You've Learned

Read and Remember

True or False Write **T** next to each sentence that is true. Write **F** next to each sentence that is false.

_____ **1)** The North had small farms and many factories.

_____ **2)** People grew cotton, sugar cane, and tobacco in the South.

_____ **3)** Slaves worked on many plantations in the North.

_____ **4)** The North said that slavery should be allowed in the West.

_____ **5)** Harriet Tubman only helped three slaves escape.

_____ **6)** Abraham Lincoln became President of the United States in 1861.

_____ **7)** Thirteen northern states left the United States and became the Confederate States of America.

_____ **8)** The Confederate States had their own constitution, flag, and money.

Think and Apply

Fact or Opinion Write **F** next to each fact below. Write **O** next to each opinion. You should find four sentences that are opinions.

_____ **1)** The North had fewer slaves than the South did.

_____ **2)** People in the South were the best farmers.

_____ **3)** The Constitution allowed slavery.

_____ **4)** People in the North should not tell people in the South what to do.

_____ **5)** Abolitionists were working to end slavery.

_____ **6)** The Fugitive Slave Act was not a good law.

_____ **7)** President Lincoln did not want slavery in the West.

_____ **8)** The southern states were wrong to leave the Union.

_____ **9)** Jefferson Davis became president of the Confederate States.

Skill Builder

Reading a Bar Graph Graphs are drawings that help you compare facts. The graph on this page is a **bar graph**. It shows facts using bars of different lengths. The bar graph below shows the number of people who lived in the United States in 1860. Study the bar graph.

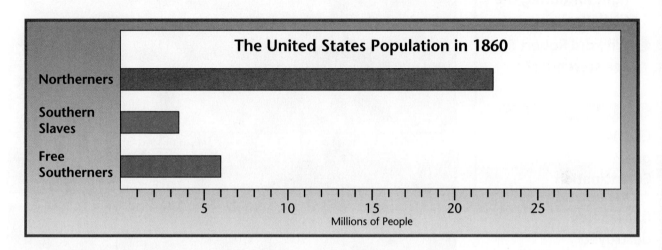

The United States Population in 1860

Northerners

Southern Slaves

Free Southerners

5   10   15   20   25

Millions of People

Draw a circle around the correct answer.

1. About how many people lived in the North?
   $3\frac{1}{2}$ million   6 million   22 million

2. About how many slaves lived in the South?
   $3\frac{1}{2}$ million   6 million   22 million

3. Which group had the largest population?
   Northerners   Free Southerners   Southern Slaves

4. Which group had about 6 million people?
   Northerners   Free Southerners   Southern Slaves

5. What was the total number of people living in the South?
   $3\frac{1}{2}$ million $9\frac{1}{2}$ million   16 million

Journal Writing

Harriet Tubman helped slaves escape. Why did she help them? Write a paragraph in your journal that tells why Tubman helped slaves.

The Civil War

NEW WORDS

Civil War
goal
Emancipation
  Proclamation
battlefields
destroyed
rebuild

PEOPLE & PLACES

Fort Sumter
Confederates
Robert E. Lee
Clara Barton
Ulysses S. Grant
Richmond

Many soldiers from both the North and the South died in the Civil War.

The South had started a new country called the Confederate States of America. President Lincoln did not want the North to fight against the South. He wanted the South to become part of the United States again. The South also did not want a war. But the South did not want to be part of the Union.

The United States Army owned a fort called Fort Sumter in South Carolina. South Carolina was one of the Confederate States. People who lived in the Confederate States were called Confederates. They said that the United States must give Fort Sumter to the Confederate States of America. But Union soldiers would not surrender Fort Sumter.

In 1861 Confederate soldiers began to shoot at Fort Sumter. A war between the North and South had begun.

Confederate battle flag

Robert E. Lee

This war was called the **Civil War**. The Civil War lasted four years. People in the South fought to have their own country, the Confederate States of America. The North fought so that all states would remain in the Union.

The Confederates thought they would win. They had many good army generals and brave soldiers. But the North was stronger than the South. The North had more people and more soldiers. The North had more money to pay for a war. The North had more railroads. Union soldiers traveled on these railroads to many places. The North had more factories, too. Northern factories made guns for the war. The South had few factories.

Robert E. Lee was the leader of the Confederate army. Lee loved the United States. He did not like slavery. He also loved his own state of Virginia. President Lincoln wanted Robert E. Lee to lead the Union army. But Lee would not fight against his family and friends in Virginia. Instead, he became the leader

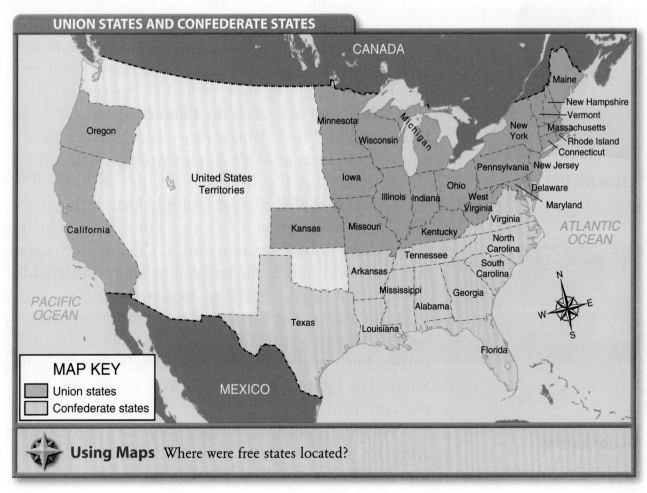

UNION STATES AND CONFEDERATE STATES

CANADA

Maine
New Hampshire
Vermont
Minnesota
Wisconsin
Michigan
New York
Massachusetts
Rhode Island
Connecticut
Oregon
Pennsylvania
New Jersey
Iowa
Ohio
Delaware
United States Territories
Illinois
Indiana
West Virginia
Maryland
California
Virginia
ATLANTIC OCEAN
Kansas
Missouri
Kentucky
North Carolina
Tennessee
South Carolina
Arkansas
PACIFIC OCEAN
Mississippi
Georgia
Alabama
Texas
Louisiana
Florida

N
W E
S

MEXICO

MAP KEY
Union states
Confederate states

Using Maps Where were free states located?

Many African Americans joined the Union army and fought in the Civil War.

Clara Barton

Major battles

of the Confederate army. General Lee was a good leader. He led the Confederate army for four long years.

President Lincoln had a **goal**. His goal was for the North and South to be one nation. He decided to help the Union win by working to end slavery. In 1862 he wrote a paper that said all slaves in the Confederate States were free. He wrote that the slaves would be free on January 1, 1863. The paper was called the **Emancipation Proclamation**. Many African American slaves left the South. Thousands of brave African Americans joined the Union army. They fought in many battles of the Civil War.

Women in the North and South helped during the war. They managed farms and factories. Some women became spies. Many women became nurses. Clara Barton was a famous Union nurse. She traveled to many **battlefields**. Clara Barton cared for soldiers who were hurt.

At the start of the Civil War, the South won many battles. After two years the South lost more and more battles. Most of the Civil War battles were fought in the South. The fighting **destroyed** houses, cities, and plantations in the South.

General Ulysses S. Grant was the leader of the Union army. He won many battles. In 1865 the Union soldiers captured Richmond, Virginia. Richmond was the

Learning from Pictures
What happened to
President Abraham
Lincoln soon after the
end of the Civil War?

PRIMARY SOURCE

"I would save the Union. I would save it the shortest way under the Constitution."

–Abraham Lincoln, 1862

capital of the Confederate States. General Lee knew the Confederates could not win the war. There was very little food to eat in the South. Lee's army was hungry. The soldiers did not have enough guns. Lee did not want more people to die in the war. Lee surrendered to Grant in April 1865. The Civil War was over. Plans were made to return the Confederate States to the Union. General Lee returned to Virginia. He told the South to help the United States become a strong country.

President Lincoln was glad that the United States was one nation again. He was also unhappy. About 600,000 soldiers in the North and South had been killed. Thousands of other soldiers were badly hurt.

President Lincoln had new goals when the war ended. He wanted Americans to work together to **rebuild** the South. Lincoln wanted Americans in the North and South to like one another again.

President Lincoln never reached these goals. He was shot five days after the Civil War ended. President Lincoln died the next day. Americans in the North and South were sad because a great leader was dead.

People in the North and the South were united once again. It would take many more years to end the anger between the North and the South. But together they would continue to make the United States a great nation.

Ulysses S. Grant

Using What You've Learned

Read and Remember

Write the Answer Write a sentence to answer each question.

1 What did the North fight for in the Civil War? _____

_____

2 What did the South fight for in the Civil War? _____

_____

3 What was the Emancipation Proclamation? _____

_____

4 How did women help during the Civil War? _____

_____

5 Why did Clara Barton travel to many battlefields during the Civil War?

_____

_____

Match Up Finish each sentence in Group A with words from Group B. Write the letter of the correct answer on the blank.

Group A

1 The Civil War began when Confederate soldiers _____

2 The leader of the Confederate army was_____

3 When President Lincoln wrote the Emancipation Proclamation, _____

4 The leader of the Union army was _____

5 Most of the Civil War battles _____

Group B

a. General Ulysses S. Grant.

b. were fought in the South.

c. General Robert E. Lee.

d. began to shoot at Fort Sumter in South Carolina.

e. many African Americans who had been slaves left the South.

Think and Apply

Sequencing Events Write the numbers 1, 2, 3, 4, and 5 next to these sentences to show the correct order.

_____ In 1862 President Lincoln wrote the Emancipation Proclamation.

_____ In 1861 Confederate soldiers attacked Fort Sumter.

_____ President Lincoln was killed after the war ended.

_____ The war ended when General Robert E. Lee surrendered to General Ulysses S. Grant.

_____ In 1865 the Union captured the Confederate capital at Richmond, Virginia.

Drawing Conclusions Read each pair of sentences. Then look in the box for the conclusion you can make. Write the letter of the conclusion on the blank.

_____ **1** The Confederates wanted Fort Sumter in South Carolina.
Union soldiers would not surrender Fort Sumter.

_____ **2** President Lincoln wanted Robert E. Lee to lead the Union army.
Lee would not fight against his family and friends in Virginia.

_____ **3** The North had more factories and soldiers than the South did.
The North had more money and railroads than the South did.

_____ **4** The Confederate soldiers did not have enough food.
The Confederate soldiers did not have enough guns.

Conclusions

a. The Confederates could not win the war.

b. The North was stronger than the South.

c. Confederate soldiers began to shoot at Fort Sumter.

d. Lee decided not to lead the Union army.

Journal Writing

The Civil War was a long, hard war between the Union and the Confederate States. Write a paragraph about the Civil War in your journal. Tell how it began or how it ended. Write at least five sentences.

Skill Builder

Reading a Table A **table** lists a group of facts. You can compare facts by reading a table. Look at the table below. It compares the North and South before the Civil War. To learn facts about the North and the South, read the numbers listed beneath each heading. Read the table from left to right to find out what the numbers in the table stand for.

The North and South Before the Civil War		
	North	South
Money	$330,000,000	$47,000,000
Number of factories and shops	111,000	21,000
Miles of railroad track	22,000	9,000
Horses	3,400,000	1,700,000
Units of wheat	132,000,000	31,000

Draw a circle around the number, word, or words that answers each question.

1 How many miles of railroad track did the South have before the Civil War?
22,000   9,000   111,000

2 How many factories and shops did the North have before the war?
3,400,000   21,000   111,000

3 How much money did the South have compared to the North before the war?
more   less   the same amount of

4 How many horses did the North have compared to the South?
more   fewer   the same number of

5 How many units of wheat for food did the North have compared to the South?
more   fewer   the same number of

6 Based on the chart, how would you compare the North to the South?
stronger than   weaker than   about the same as

Review

Study the time line on this page. Then use the words in blue print to finish the story. Write the words you choose on the correct blank line.

slaves   Lincoln   state
Texas   California   Lee
Cession   Confederate   Civil War

In 1836 **(1)** _____ won a war for independence from Mexico. In 1845 Texas became a **(2)** _____ . The United States fought a war with Mexico. From that war the United States got the Mexican **(3)** _____ . Many Americans moved west. After the gold rush, **(4)** _____ became a state in 1850.

As the nation grew larger, the North and the South quarreled about slavery. In 1861 southern states started a new nation called the **(5)** _____ States of America. Later that year, the **(6)** _____ began. President Abraham Lincoln wrote the Emancipation Proclamation. This paper said that **(7)** _____ in the Confederate States were free. In 1865 General **(8)** _____ surrendered to General Grant. The Union had won the Civil War. A few days later, **(9)** _____ was killed.

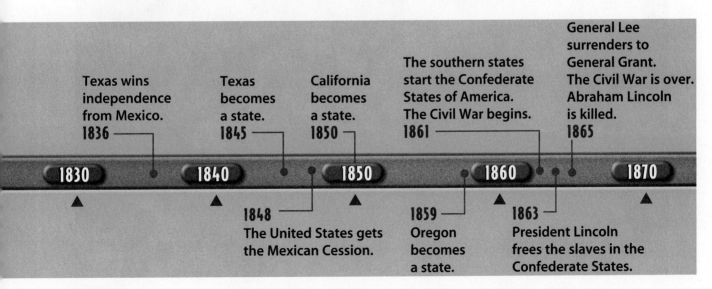

Texas wins independence from Mexico. 1836

Texas becomes a state. 1845

California becomes a state. 1850

The southern states start the Confederate States of America. The Civil War begins. 1861

General Lee surrenders to General Grant. The Civil War is over. Abraham Lincoln is killed. 1865

1830   1840   1850   1860   1870

1848
The United States gets the Mexican Cession.

1859
Oregon becomes a state.

1863
President Lincoln frees the slaves in the Confederate States.

THE UNITED STATES

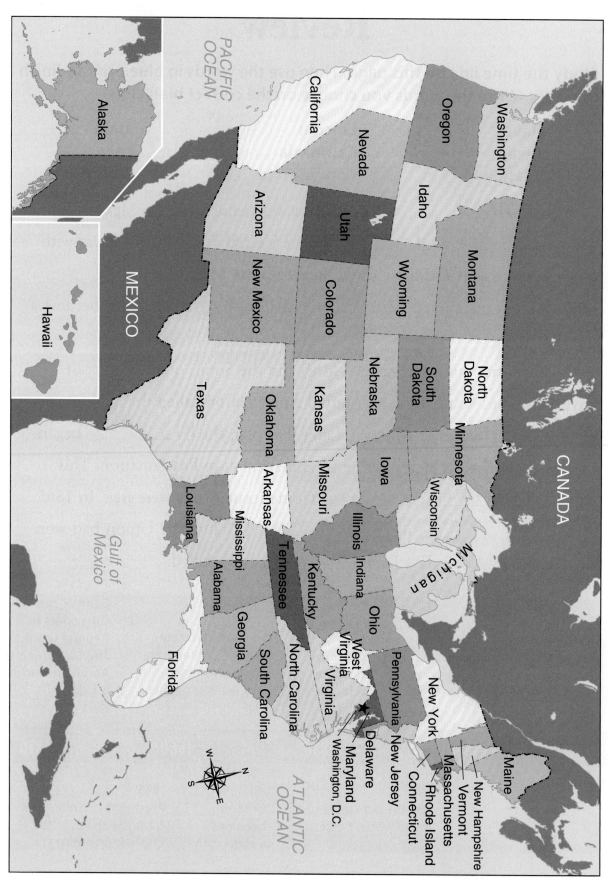

THE UNITED STATES: LANDFORMS

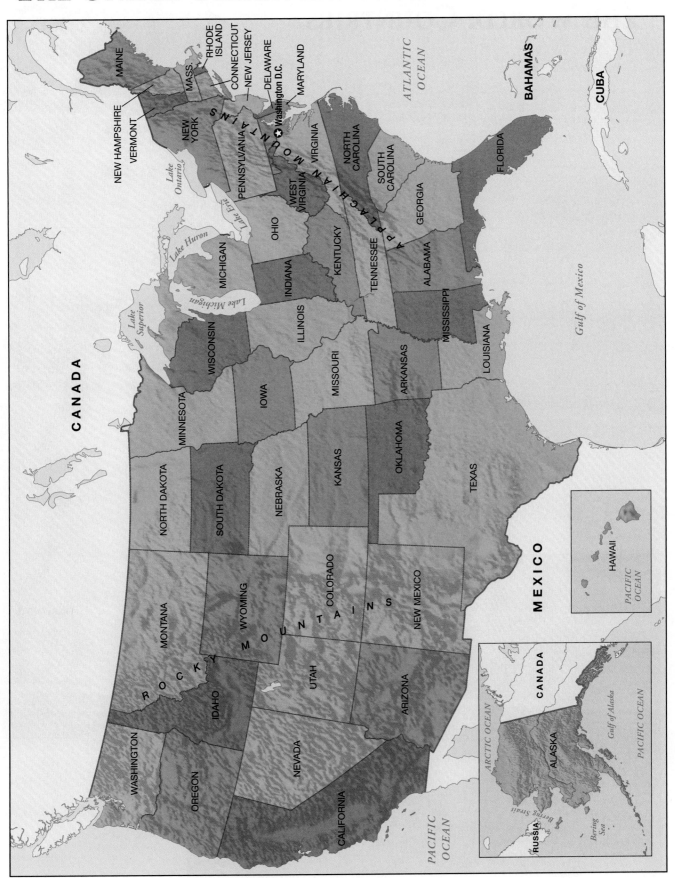

CANADA

MAINE

NEW HAMPSHIRE
VERMONT

MASS.

RHODE ISLAND
CONNECTICUT
NEW JERSEY
DELAWARE
MARYLAND

Washington D.C.

ATLANTIC OCEAN

BAHAMAS

CUBA

NEW YORK

PENNSYLVANIA

Lake Ontario

Lake Erie

WEST VIRGINIA

VIRGINIA

NORTH CAROLINA

SOUTH CAROLINA

FLORIDA

Lake Huron

OHIO

KENTUCKY

TENNESSEE

GEORGIA

Lake Superior

MICHIGAN

Lake Michigan

INDIANA

ALABAMA

APPALACHIAN MOUNTAINS

Gulf of Mexico

WISCONSIN

ILLINOIS

MISSISSIPPI

MINNESOTA

IOWA

MISSOURI

ARKANSAS

LOUISIANA

NORTH DAKOTA

SOUTH DAKOTA

NEBRASKA

KANSAS

OKLAHOMA

TEXAS

MEXICO

HAWAII

PACIFIC OCEAN

COLORADO

NEW MEXICO

WYOMING

R O C K Y   M O U N T A I N S

MONTANA

IDAHO

UTAH

ARIZONA

WASHINGTON

OREGON

NEVADA

CALIFORNIA

PACIFIC OCEAN

CANADA

ARCTIC OCEAN

Gulf of Alaska

PACIFIC OCEAN

ALASKA

Bering Strait

RUSSIA

Bering Sea

147

THE WORLD: COUNTRIES

Alaska (U.S.)

CANADA

NORTH AMERICA

UNITED STATES

PACIFIC OCEAN

Hawaii (U.S.)

MEXICO

ATLANTIC OCEAN

See inset below

VENEZUELA

COLOMBIA

GALAPAGOS IS. (ECUADOR)

ECUADOR

GUYANA
SURINAME
FRENCH GUIANA

SOUTH AMERICA

PERU

BRAZIL

SAMOA ISLANDS

FRENCH POLYNESIA (FRANCE)

BOLIVIA

PARAGUAY

URUGUAY

PACIFIC OCEAN

CHILE

ARGENTINA

FALKLAND IS. (U.K.)

Inset

U.S.

Gulf of Mexico

BAHAMAS

ATLANTIC OCEAN

CUBA

Turks & Caicos Islands (U.K.)

MEXICO

Cayman Islands (U.K.)

Virgin Islands (U.S.)

Virgin Islands (U.K.)

HAITI

DOMINICAN REPUBLIC

JAMAICA

Puerto Rico (U.S.)

ST. KITTS AND NEVIS

ANTIGUA & BARBUDA

Guadeloupe (France)

DOMINICA

Martinique (France)

ST. LUCIA

GUATEMALA

BELIZE

HONDURAS

Caribbean Sea

NICARAGUA

EL SALVADOR

COSTA RICA

Panama Canal

ARUBA (Neth.)

NETHERLANDS ANTILLES (Neth.)

ST. VINCENT AND THE GRENADINES

BARBADOS

GRENADA

TRINIDAD & TOBAGO

PACIFIC OCEAN

PANAMA

COLOMBIA

VENEZUELA

GUYANA

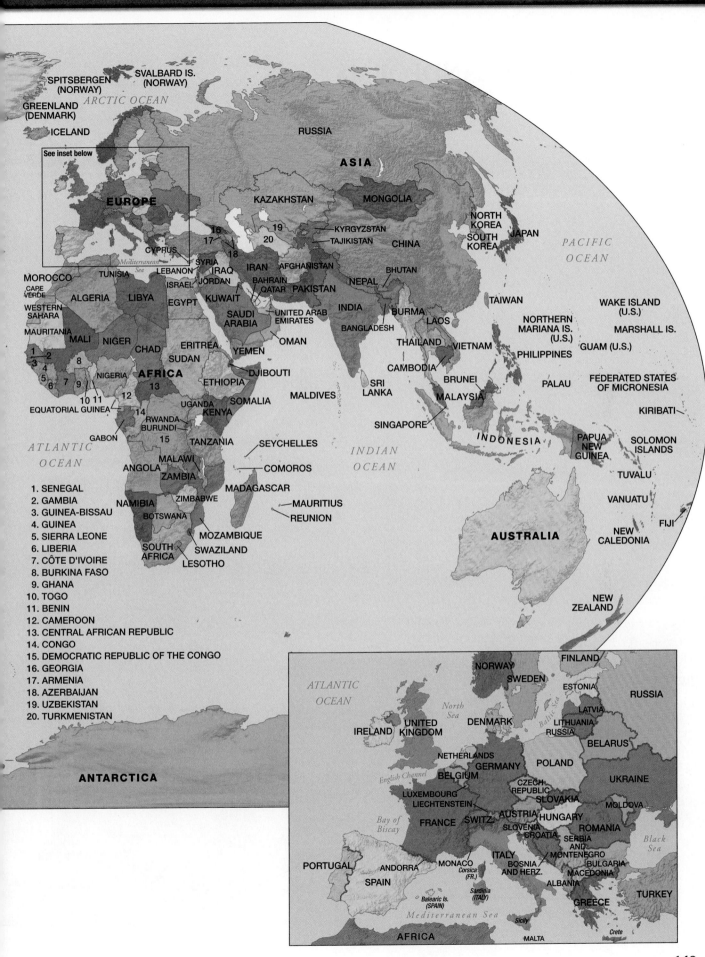

SPITSBERGEN
(NORWAY)

SVALBARD IS.
(NORWAY)

ARCTIC OCEAN

GREENLAND
(DENMARK)

ICELAND

See inset below

EUROPE

RUSSIA

ASIA

KAZAKHSTAN

MONGOLIA

NORTH
KOREA

SOUTH
KOREA

JAPAN

*PACIFIC
OCEAN*

KYRGYZSTAN

TAJIKISTAN

CHINA

CYPRUS

*Mediterranean
Sea*

16

17

18

19

20

SYRIA
LEBANON

IRAN

AFGHANISTAN

BHUTAN

TAIWAN

WAKE ISLAND
(U.S.)

MOROCCO

TUNISIA

ISRAEL
JORDAN

IRAQ

QATAR

PAKISTAN

NEPAL

NORTHERN
MARIANA IS.
(U.S.)

MARSHALL IS.

CAPE
VERDE

ALGERIA

LIBYA

EGYPT

KUWAIT

BAHRAIN

UNITED ARAB
EMIRATES

INDIA

BURMA

LAOS

GUAM (U.S.)

WESTERN
SAHARA

SAUDI
ARABIA

BANGLADESH

THAILAND

VIETNAM

PHILIPPINES

FEDERATED STATES
OF MICRONESIA

MAURITANIA

MALI

NIGER

CHAD

OMAN

YEMEN

CAMBODIA

BRUNEI

PALAU

1
2
3
4
5
6

8

ERITREA

SUDAN

DJIBOUTI

SRI
LANKA

MALAYSIA

KIRIBATI

NIGERIA

AFRICA

13

ETHIOPIA

MALDIVES

7
9

10 11

12

SOMALIA

UGANDA

KENYA

SINGAPORE

INDONESIA

PAPUA
NEW
GUINEA

SOLOMON
ISLANDS

EQUATORIAL GUINEA

14

RWANDA
BURUNDI

15

TANZANIA

SEYCHELLES

*INDIAN

OCEAN*

TUVALU

GABON

*ATLANTIC

OCEAN*

MALAWI

ANGOLA

ZAMBIA

COMOROS

MADAGASCAR

VANUATU

1. SENEGAL
2. GAMBIA
3. GUINEA-BISSAU
4. GUINEA
5. SIERRA LEONE
6. LIBERIA
7. CÔTE D'IVOIRE
8. BURKINA FASO
9. GHANA
10. TOGO
11. BENIN
12. CAMEROON
13. CENTRAL AFRICAN REPUBLIC
14. CONGO
15. DEMOCRATIC REPUBLIC OF THE CONGO
16. GEORGIA
17. ARMENIA
18. AZERBAIJAN
19. UZBEKISTAN
20. TURKMENISTAN

NAMIBIA

ZIMBABWE

BOTSWANA

MOZAMBIQUE

SWAZILAND

SOUTH
AFRICA

LESOTHO

MAURITIUS

REUNION

NEW
CALEDONIA

FIJI

AUSTRALIA

NEW
ZEALAND

ANTARCTICA

NORWAY

FINLAND

*ATLANTIC

OCEAN*

SWEDEN

ESTONIA

RUSSIA

*North
Sea*

DENMARK

LATVIA

*Baltic
Sea*

LITHUANIA

RUSSIA

BELARUS

IRELAND

UNITED
KINGDOM

NETHERLANDS

GERMANY

POLAND

UKRAINE

English Channel

BELGIUM

CZECH
REPUBLIC

LUXEMBOURG

LIECHTENSTEIN

SLOVAKIA

MOLDOVA

*Bay of
Biscay*

FRANCE

SWITZ.

AUSTRIA

HUNGARY

ROMANIA

SLOVENIA

CROATIA

SERBIA
AND
MONTENEGRO

*Black
Sea*

PORTUGAL

ANDORRA

MONACO

*Corsica
(FR.)*

ITALY

BOSNIA
AND HERZ.

BULGARIA

SPAIN

*Balearic Is.
(SPAIN)*

*Sardinia
(ITALY)*

MACEDONIA

ALBANIA

TURKEY

GREECE

Mediterranean Sea

Sicily

Crete

AFRICA

MALTA

149

THE WORLD: LANDFORMS

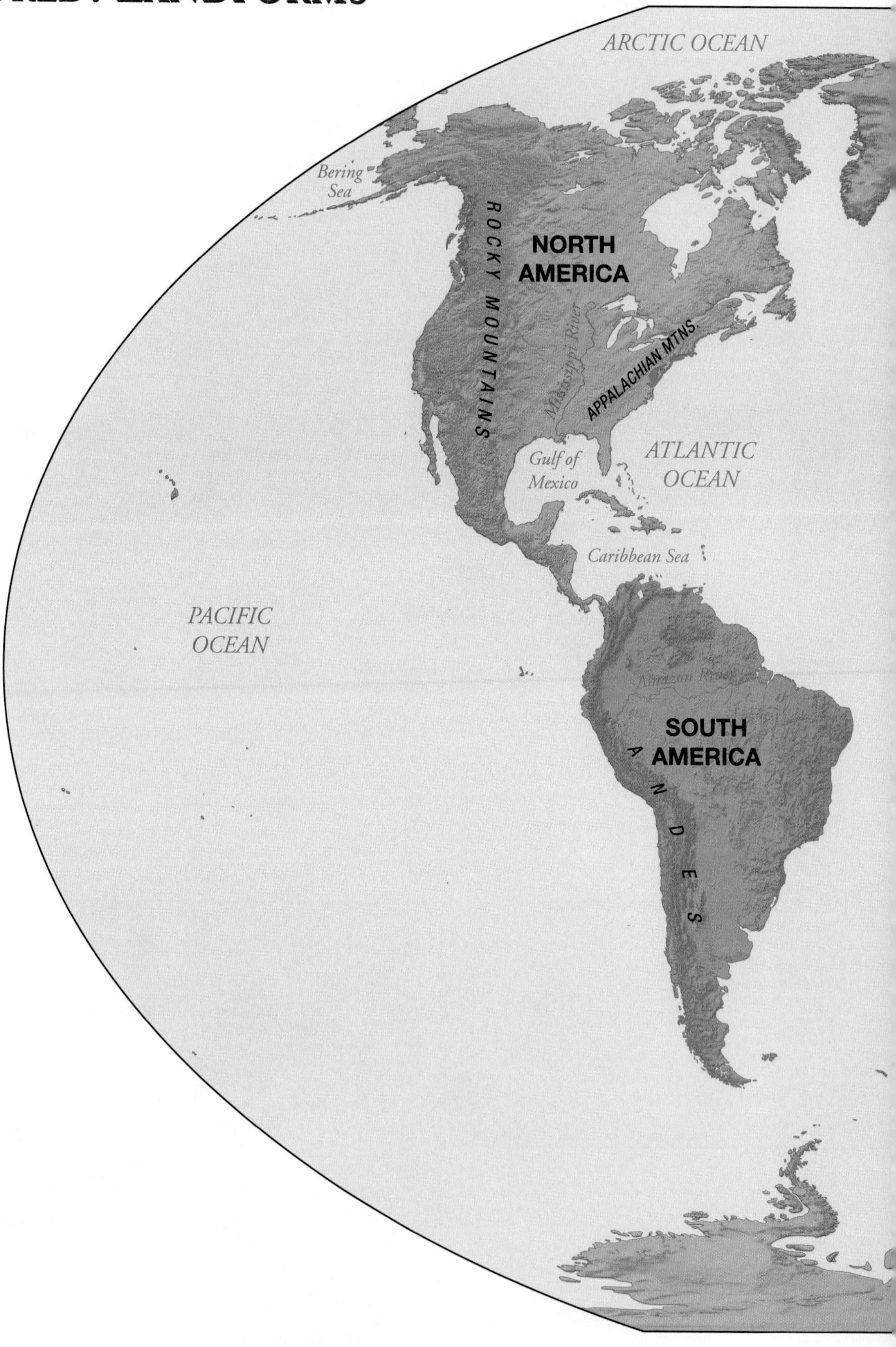

ARCTIC OCEAN

Bering
Sea

ROCKY MOUNTAINS

NORTH
AMERICA

Mississippi River

APPALACHIAN MTNS.

Gulf of
Mexico

ATLANTIC
OCEAN

Caribbean Sea

PACIFIC
OCEAN

Amazon River

SOUTH
AMERICA

A
N
D
E
S

ARCTIC OCEAN

URAL MOUNTAINS

EUROPE

ASIA

ALPS

Danube River

Hwang He

Mediterranean Sea

HIMALAYAS

Chang Jiang

Indus River

Ganges River

Niger River

Arabian
Sea

AFRICA

PACIFIC
OCEAN

INDIAN OCEAN

AUSTRALIA

Darling River

ANTARCTICA

151

Declaration of Independence

When in the course of human events, it becomes necessary for one people to dissolve the political bands which have connected them with another, and to assume among the powers of the earth the separate and equal station to which the laws of nature and of nature's God entitle them, a decent respect to the opinions of mankind requires that they should declare the causes which impel them to the separation.

Sometimes in history one group of people may want to be free from the country that rules it. The group must tell the world why. That is the reason for the Declaration of Independence.

We hold these truths to be self-evident: that all men are created equal, that they are endowed by their Creator with certain unalienable rights, that among these are life, liberty, and the pursuit of happiness.

We believe some things are always true. All people are equal. God gave all people rights that other people should not be able to take away. These rights include life, freedom, and the chance to be happy.

That to secure these rights, governments are instituted among men, deriving their just powers from the consent of the governed; that whenever any form of government becomes destructive of these ends, it is the right of the people to alter or to abolish it, and to institute new government, laying its foundation on such principles and organizing its powers in such form as to them shall seem most likely to effect their safety and happiness. Prudence, indeed, will dictate that governments long established should not be changed for light and transient causes; and accordingly all experience hath shown, that mankind are more disposed to suffer while evils are sufferable, than to right themselves by abolishing the forms to which they are accustomed. But when a long train of abuses and usurpations, pursuing invariably the same object, evinces a design to reduce them under absolute despotism, it is their right, it is their duty, to throw off such government, and to provide new guards for their future security.

People make governments to keep their rights safe. People agree to give governments power. If the governments do a poor job, the people can change or end the government. Governments should not be changed for small reasons. But when a government treats its people very badly, the people must put an end to the government. The people can start a new government.

Such has been the patient sufferance of these colonies; and such is now the necessity which constrains them to alter their former systems of government. The history of the present king of Great Britain is a history of repeated injuries and usurpations, all having in direct object the establishment of an absolute tyranny over these states. To prove this, let facts be submitted to a candid world.

For a long time, the colonies have been treated badly by the king's government. This is why they need to change their government. King George has hurt the colonies again and again. His goal is to control the colonies. We want the world to know these facts:

He has refused his assent to laws, the most wholesome and necessary for the public good.

The king does not make laws that are good for the colonies.

He has forbidden his governors to pass laws of immediate and pressing importance, unless suspended in their operation till his assent should be obtained, and when so suspended, he has utterly neglected to attend to them.

The king will not let us make our own laws. He takes too much time to agree to the ones he thinks are good.

He has refused to pass other laws for the accommodation of large districts of people, unless those people would relinquish the right of representation in the legislature, a right inestimable to them and formidable to tyrants only.

He has not let us have our leaders speak for us.

He has called together legislative bodies at places unusual, uncomfortable, and distant from the depository of their public records, for the sole purpose of fatiguing them into compliance with his measures.

He has made leaders meet in strange, uncomfortable, and far away places. He hopes leaders will become tired and obey his orders.

He has dissolved Representative Houses repeatedly, for opposing with manly firmness his invasions on the rights of the people.

He has closed meetings of leaders in the colonies when they say the king has treated the people badly.

He has refused for a long time, after such dissolutions, to cause others to be elected; whereby the legislative powers, incapable of annihilation, have returned to the people at large for their exercise; the state remaining, in the mean time, exposed to all the dangers of invasion from without, and convulsions within.

He has taken a long time to allow elections. The colonists were in danger because they could not make laws to keep them safe.

He has endeavored to prevent the population of these states; for that purpose obstructing the laws of naturalization of foreigners, refusing to pass others to encourage their migration hither, and raising the conditions of new appropriations of lands.

King George has tried to stop the colonies from growing. He would not allow other Europeans to settle in the colonies. He has made it hard to buy land in America.

He has obstructed the administration of justice, by refusing his assent to laws for establishing judiciary powers.

He would not let us set up courts.

He has made judges dependent on his will alone, for the tenure of their offices, and the amount and payment of their salaries.

The king pays the judges. They make unfair decisions to keep their jobs.

He has erected a multitude of new offices, and sent hither swarms of officers to harass our people, and eat out their substance.

The king has sent many government people. They bother us and use up our supplies.

He has kept among us, in times of peace, standing armies without the consent of our legislatures.

The king has kept his armies here and we do not want them.

He has affected to render the military independent of and superior to the civil power.

He has tried to make his armies more powerful than our government.

He has combined with others to subject us to a jurisdiction foreign to our constitution, and unacknowledged by our laws; giving his assent to their acts of pretended legislation:

King George has worked with Parliament to make unfair laws that we did not help write.

For quartering large bodies of armed troops among us;

They made us let British soldiers stay in our homes.

For protecting them, by a mock trial, from punishment for any murders which they should commit on the inhabitants of these states;

British soldiers who killed our colonists went free without real trials.

For cutting off our trade with all parts of the world;

They stopped us from trading with other countries.

For imposing taxes on us without our consent;

They made unfair tax laws for us.

For depriving us, in many cases, of the benefits of trial by jury;

They often took away our right to have a fair trial.

For transporting us beyond seas to be tried for pretended offenses;

They made some of us go to Great Britain to go on trial for made-up crimes.

For abolishing the free system of English laws in a neighboring province, establishing therein an arbitrary government, and enlarging its boundaries so as to render it at once an example and fit instrument for introducing the same absolute rule into these colonies;

They took away the fair government of an area that is our neighbor. They gave them an unfair government. This was to show us how Great Britain can have complete rule over the colonies.

For taking away our charters, abolishing our most valuable laws, and altering fundamentally the forms of our governments;

They took away our land agreements. They changed our most important laws. They changed our government.

For suspending our own legislatures, and declaring themselves invested with power to legislate for us in all cases whatsoever.

They have stopped our leaders from making laws. They say they have the power to make all our laws.

He has abdicated government here, by declaring us out of his protection and waging war against us.

King George has given up his power to rule us because he does not keep us safe. He says he is fighting a war against us.

He has plundered our seas, ravaged our coasts, burnt our towns, and destroyed the lives of our people.

The king has attacked our ships and destroyed our ports. He has burned our towns and destroyed our lives.

He is at this time transporting large armies of foreign mercenaries to complete the works of death, desolation, and tyranny, already begun with circumstances of cruelty and perfidy scarcely paralleled in the most barbarous ages, and totally unworthy the head of a civilized nation.

He is bringing soldiers from other countries to destroy the colonies. A modern king should not allow soldiers to be so horrible.

He has constrained our fellow citizens taken captive on the high seas to bear arms against their country, to become the executioners of their friends and brethren, or to fall themselves by their hands.

He has taken Americans off our ships at sea. He has made them fight against other Americans.

He has excited domestic insurrections amongst us, and has endeavored to bring on the inhabitants of our frontiers, the merciless Indian savages, whose known rule of warfare, is an undistinguished destruction of all ages, sexes and conditions.

He has told those who work for us to fight against us. He has tried to get Native Americans to attack us.

In every stage of these oppressions we have petitioned for redress in the most humble terms; our repeated petitions have been answered only by repeated injury. A prince whose character is thus marked by every act which may define a tyrant is unfit to be the ruler of a free people.

We have asked the king to stop treating us unfairly. But he has only made things harder for us. A king who acts so unfairly is not good enough to rule a free people.

Nor have we been wanting in attentions to our British brethren. We have warned them from time to time of attempts by their legislature to extend an unwarrantable jurisdiction over us. We have reminded them of the circumstances of our emigration and settlement here. We have appealed to their native justice and magnanimity, and we have conjured them by the ties of our common kindred to disavow these usurpations, which would inevitably interrupt our connections and correspondence. They too have been deaf to the voice of justice and of consanguinity. We must, therefore, acquiesce in the necessity which denounces our separation, and hold them, as we hold the rest of mankind, enemies in war, in peace friends.

We have told the British people many times how poorly Parliament has treated us. We hoped they would help us. But they did not listen to us. Now we must say that we are a separate nation. We will treat Great Britain as we treat all other nations.

We, therefore, the representatives of the United States of America, in General Congress assembled, appealing to the Supreme Judge of the world for the rectitude of our intentions, do, in the name, and by authority of the good people of these colonies, solemnly publish and declare, that these united colonies are, and of right ought to be, free and independent states; that they are absolved from all allegiance to the British crown, and that all political connection between them and the state of Great Britain is, and ought to be, totally dissolved; and that as free and

independent states, they have full power to levy war, conclude peace, contract alliances, establish commerce, and to do all other acts and things which independent states may of right do.

As leaders of the people of the United States, we say that these colonies are united as an independent nation. We have no more ties to Great Britain. As an independent nation, we have the right to make war. We have the right to make peace treaties. We have the right to trade with all nations. We have the right to do all the things a nation does.

And for the support of this declaration, with a firm reliance on the protection of Divine Providence, we mutually pledge to each other our lives, our fortunes and our sacred honor.

We now trust that God will keep us safe. We promise our lives, our money, and our honor for this Declaration.

John Hancock
(President,
Massachusetts)

Georgia
Button Gwinnett
Lyman Hall
George Walton

North Carolina
William Hooper
Joseph Hewes
John Penn

South Carolina
Edward Rutledge
Thomas Heyward, Jr.
Thomas Lynch, Jr.
Arthur Middleton

Maryland
Samuel Chase

William Paca
Thomas Stone
Charles Carroll of
Carrollton

Virginia
George Wythe
Richard Henry Lee
Thomas Jefferson
Benjamin Harrison
Thomas Nelson, Jr.
Francis Lightfoot Lee
Carter Braxton

Pennsylvania
Robert Morris
Benjamin Rush
Benjamin Franklin
John Morton
George Clymer
James Smith

George Taylor
James Wilson
George Ross

Delaware
Caesar Rodney
George Read
Thomas McKean

New York
William Floyd
Philip Livingston
Francis Lewis
Lewis Morris

New Jersey
Richard Stockton
John Witherspoon
Francis Hopkinson
John Hart
Abraham Clark

New Hampshire
Josiah Bartlett
William Whipple
Matthew Thornton

Massachusetts
John Adams
Samuel Adams
Robert Treat Paine
Elbridge Gerry

Rhode Island
Stephen Hopkins
William Ellery

Connecticut
Roger Sherman
Samuel Huntington
William Williams
Oliver Wolcott

The Constitution
of the United States of America

PREAMBLE

We, the People of the United States, in order to form a more perfect Union, establish justice, insure domestic tranquility, provide for the common defense, promote the general welfare, and secure the blessings of liberty to ourselves and our posterity, do ordain and establish this Constitution for the United States of America.

The Constitution is a set of laws for the United States. The first part of the Constitution is called the Preamble. It starts with the words "We the people of the United States." This means the laws were made by the American people and not by a king. It also means the laws are for all the states. The states form one nation. The Preamble tells us the goals of the Constitution. The goals are to create a strong government that will help people have peace and freedom.

ARTICLE I. THE LEGISLATIVE BRANCH

Section 1. The Congress

All legislative powers herein granted shall be vested in a Congress of the United States, which shall consist of a Senate and House of Representatives.

The Constitution separates the government's powers into three branches. This is called the **separation of powers**. The writers of the Constitution did not want any person or any part of government to have too much power. With too much power, a leader could take away freedom from the people. The writers remembered how King George had used his power to take away American freedom. They did not want Americans to have that kind of problem again. So they gave Congress the power to make laws. Article 1 tells about the powers of Congress. Congress is the **legislative** [lawmaking] branch of the government. Only Congress can write laws for the United States. Congress gets its power from the American people. Americans vote for the people who will represent them in Congress.

Congress has two parts. Each part is called a house. The Senate and the House of Representatives are the two houses of Congress.

Section 2. The House of Representatives

The House of Representatives shall be composed of members chosen every second year by the people of the several states, and the electors in each state shall have the qualifications requisite for electors of the most numerous branch of the state legislature.

Once in two years, Americans vote for people in their state to be members of the House of Representatives. Members serve two-year terms.

No person shall be a Representative who shall not have attained the age of 25 years, and been seven years a citizen of the United States, and who shall not, when elected, be an inhabitant of that state in which he shall be chosen.

To work in the House, a person must be 25 years old. A person must be an American citizen for seven years. All members of the House must live in the state that they represent.

~~Representatives and direct taxes shall be apportioned among the several states which may be included within this Union, according to their respective numbers, which shall be determined by adding to the whole number of free persons, including those bound to service for a term of years, and excluding Indians not taxed, three fifths of all other persons.~~ The actual enumeration shall be made within three years after the first meeting of the Congress of the United States, and within every subsequent term of ten years, in such manner as they shall by law direct. The number of Representatives shall not exceed one for every 30,000, but each state shall have at least one Representative; and until such enumeration shall be made, the state of New Hampshire shall be entitled to choose three, Massachusetts eight, Rhode Island and Providence Plantations one, Connecticut five, New York six, New Jersey four, Pennsylvania eight, Delaware one, Maryland six, Virginia ten, North Carolina five, South Carolina five, and Georgia three.

States with large populations send more people to work in the House of Representatives. States with smaller populations send fewer people to work in the House. Every ten years there must be a **census** [a counting of all people in the country by government workers]. When a state's population changes, the number of representatives that a state sends to Congress changes.

When vacancies happen in the representation from any state, the executive authority thereof shall issue writs of election to fill such vacancies.

The House of Representatives shall choose their Speaker and other officers; and shall have the sole power of impeachment.

The members of the House of Representatives must vote for a leader. The leader is called the Speaker of the House. The House of Representatives is the only part of the government that can **impeach** [accuse] a government leader for doing things wrongly. Only two presidents, Andrew Johnson and Bill Clinton, were impeached.

Section 3. The Senate

The Senate of the United States shall be composed of two Senators from each state, ~~chosen by the legislature thereof,~~ for six years; and each Senator shall have one vote.

Every state, large or small, sends two senators to make laws in the United States Senate. Senators serve six-year terms. In 1913, the Seventeenth Amendment was passed. It gave Americans the right to vote for their United States Senators.

Immediately after they shall be assembled in consequence of the first election, they shall be divided as equally as may be into three classes. The seats of the Senators of the first class shall be vacated at the expiration of the second year, of the second class at the expiration of the fourth year, and of the third class at the expiration of the sixth year, so that one third may be chosen every second year; ~~and if vacancies happen by resignation, or otherwise, during the recess of the legislature of any state, the executive thereof may make temporary appointments until the next meeting of the legislature, which shall then fill such vacancies.~~

No person shall be a Senator who shall not have attained the age of thirty years, and been nine years a citizen of the United States, and who shall not, when elected, be an inhabitant of that state for which he shall be chosen.

To become a senator, a person must be 30 years old. The person must be a citizen for at least nine years. All senators must live in the states that they represent.

The Vice President of the United States shall be President of the Senate, but shall have no vote, unless they be equally divided.

The Vice President of the United States works as President of the Senate. He can vote only to break a **tie vote** [an equal number of votes that are for and against a law the Senate is working on]. Senators must vote for people to be leaders of the Senate.

The Senate shall choose their other officers, and also a President *pro tempore*, in the absence of the Vice President, or when he shall exercise the office of President of the United States.

The Senate shall have the sole power to try all impeachments. When sitting for that purpose, they shall be on oath or affirmation. When the President of the United States is tried, the Chief Justice shall preside: and no person shall be convicted without the concurrence of two thirds of the members present.

Judgment in cases of impeachment shall not extend further than to removal from office, and disqualification to hold and enjoy any office of honor, trust, or profit, under the United States: but the party convicted shall nevertheless be liable and subject to indictment, trial, judgment, and punishment, according to law.

If the House of Representatives impeaches a government leader, there must be a trial in the Senate to decide if a government leader is guilty of doing things wrongly. The **Chief Justice** [leader] of the Supreme Court is the judge at trials in the Senate. If a government leader is found guilty during a Senate trial, the leader loses his job. Since 1789, only seven people have been found guilty during Senate trials. The seven guilty people were judges.

Section 4. Elections
The times, places, and manner of holding elections for Senators and

Representatives, shall be prescribed in each state by the legislature thereof; but the Congress may at any time by law make or alter such regulations, except as to the places of choosing Senators.

States can make their own rules about voting for members of Congress. Congress has the power to change state voting laws.

Elections for Congress must be on a Tuesday in early November in every state.

The Congress shall assemble at least once in every year, ~~and such meeting shall be on the first Monday in December, unless they shall by law appoint a different day~~.

Congress must meet at least once a year.

Section 5. Meetings of Congress

Each House shall be the judge of the elections, returns, and qualifications of its own members, and a majority of each shall constitute a quorum to do business; but a smaller number may adjourn from day to day, and may be authorized to compel the attendance of absent members, in such manner, and under such penalties as each House may provide.

The House of Representatives and the Senate write their own rules. They make rules about how many members must be at meetings when there will be voting on **bills** [the ideas for new laws]. Members can be punished if they miss too many meetings.

Each House may determine the rules of its proceedings, punish its members for disorderly behavior, and, with the concurrence of two thirds, expel a member.

Each house has its own rules about **debate** [talking about problems]. Senators are allowed to talk for a long time. Members of the House of Representatives can talk for only a short time.

Each House shall keep a journal of its proceedings, and from time to time publish the same, excepting such parts as may in their judgment require secrecy; and the yeas and nays of the members of either House on any question, shall, at the desire of one fifth of those present, be entered on the journal.

Both the Senate and the House of Representatives must keep journals. The journals tell what happened at meetings. They show how members voted for different bills. The journals of Congress are called *The Congressional Record*. Everyone can read these journals in public libraries. These journals help Americans decide if members of Congress are doing a good job.

Neither House, during the session of Congress, shall, without the consent of the other, adjourn for more than three days, nor to any other place than that in which the two Houses shall be sitting.

Section 6. Salaries and Rules

The Senators and Representatives shall receive a compensation for their services, to be ascertained by law, and paid out of the Treasury of the United States. They shall in all cases, except treason, felony, and breach of the peace, be privileged from arrest during their attendance at the session of their respective Houses, and in going to and returning from the same; and for any speech or debate in either House, they shall not be questioned in any other place.

Members of the Senate and the House of Representatives must be paid salaries. The writers of the Constitution wanted members of Congress to be paid so that poor people as well as rich people would have enough money to be members.

No Senator or Representative shall, during the time for which he was elected, be appointed to any civil office under the authority of the United States, which shall have been created, or the emoluments whereof shall have been increased during such time; and no person holding any office under the United States, shall be a member of either House during his continuance in office.

Members of Congress cannot hold other government jobs while serving in Congress. This rule was written so that there would be a separation of powers between the three branches of government. This rule stops members of Congress from working for the other branches.

Section 7. Bills

All bills for raising revenue shall originate in the House of Representatives; but the Senate may propose or concur with amendments as on other bills.

All tax bills must be written and then passed by the House of Representatives. Then the tax bills are sent to the Senate. The Senate must pass the tax bills in order for them to become laws.

Every bill which shall have passed the House of Representatives and the Senate, shall, before it become a law, be presented to the President of the United States; if he approve he shall sign it, but if not he shall return it, with his objections, to that House in which it shall have originated, who shall enter the objections at large on their journal, and proceed to reconsider it. If after such reconsideration two thirds of that House shall agree to pass the bill, it shall be sent, together with the objections, to the other House, by which it shall likewise be reconsidered, and if approved by two thirds of that House, it shall become a law. But in all such cases the votes of both Houses shall be determined by yeas and nays, and the names of the persons voting for and against the bill shall be entered on the journal of each House respectively. If any bill shall not be returned by the President within ten days (Sundays excepted) after it shall have been presented to him, the same shall be a law, in like manner as if he had signed it, unless the Congress by their adjournment prevent its return, in which case it shall not be a law.

Congress must obey rules when writing new laws. The first step when writing laws is for the House or Senate to write a bill that has the ideas for the new law. Then both the House and the Senate must vote to **pass** [approve] the bill. After that the bill must be sent to the President. The bill becomes a law if the President signs it. Sometimes a President feels the new law will hurt the country. He may not want the bill to become a law. So the President can **veto** [refuse to sign] the bill. But that bill can still become a law. The bill must be sent back to Congress. It can become a law if two thirds of the members of both houses vote for it.

Every order, resolution, or vote, to which the concurrence of the Senate and House of Representatives may be necessary (except on a question of adjournment), shall be presented to the President of the United States; and before the same shall take effect, shall be approved by him, or being disapproved by him, shall be repassed by two thirds of the Senate and House of Representatives, according to the rules and limitations prescribed in the case of a bill.

Section 8. Powers of Congress

The Congress shall have power:

To lay and collect taxes, duties, imposts, and excises, to pay the debts and provide for the common defense and general welfare of the United States; but all duties, imposts, and excises shall be uniform throughout the United States;

To borrow money on the credit of the United States;

To regulate commerce with foreign nations, and among the several states, and with the Indian tribes;

To establish a uniform rule of naturalization, and uniform laws on the subject of bankruptcies throughout the United States;

To coin money, regulate the value thereof, and of foreign coin, and fix the standard of weights and measures;

To provide for the punishment of counterfeiting the securities and current coin of the United States;

To establish post offices and post roads;

To promote the progress of science and useful arts, by securing for limited times to authors and inventors the exclusive right to their respective writings and discoveries;

To constitute tribunals inferior to the Supreme Court;

To define and punish piracies and felonies committed on the high seas, and offenses against the law of nations;

To declare war, grant letters of marque and reprisal, and make rules concerning captures on land and water;

To raise and support armies; but no appropriation of money to that use shall be for a longer term than two years;

To provide and maintain a navy;

To make rules for the government and regulation of the land and naval forces;

To provide for calling forth the militia to execute the laws of the Union, suppress insurrections and repel invasions;

To provide for organizing, arming, and disciplining the militia, and for governing such part of them as may be employed in the service of the United States, reserving to the states respectively, the appointment of the officers, and the authority of training the militia according to the discipline prescribed by Congress;

To exercise exclusive legislation, in all cases whatsoever, over such district (not exceeding ten miles square) as may, by cession of particular states, and the acceptance of Congress, become the seat of the government of the United States, and to exercise like authority over all places purchased by the consent of the legislature of the state in which the same shall be, for the erection of forts, magazines, arsenals, dockyards, and other needful buildings. And,

To make all laws which shall be necessary and proper for carrying into execution the foregoing powers, and all other powers vested by this Constitution in the government of the United States, or in any department or officer thereof.

Congress has all of these powers:

1. Congress makes tax laws. Congress can collect taxes. Taxes pay for highways, national parks, the army, and many other things.

2. Congress can borrow money. One of the ways it borrows money is by selling savings bonds.

3. Congress writes laws about trade between the states. It writes laws about trade with other nations.

4. Congress writes laws about how people from other countries can become American citizens.

5. Congress writes laws about printing money and making coins.

6. Congress sets up different kinds of courts.

7. Congress approves treaties with other countries.

8. Congress can **declare war** [decide that the United States will go to war] against another country.

9. Congress can form an army and a navy. Congress decides how much money to give the army and navy.

10. Congress can form a **National Guard** [soldiers to protect Americans in the United States].

Congress can write all the laws it needs to carry out its powers. This is a very important rule in the Constitution. This rule allows Congress to write laws that help the United States as the country grows and changes. The Constitution has been the law of the United States for more than 225 years because Congress has the power to always write the new laws the nation needs.

Section 9. Powers Not Given to Congress

The migration or importation of such persons as any of the states now existing shall think proper to admit, shall not be prohibited by the Congress prior to the year 1808; but a tax or duty may be imposed on such importation, not exceeding ten dollars for each person.

The privilege of the writ of *habeas corpus* shall not be suspended, unless when in cases of rebellion or invasion the public safety may require it.

No bill of attainder or *ex post facto* law shall be passed.

No capitation, or other direct tax, shall be laid, unless in proportion to the census or enumeration herein before directed to be taken.

No tax or duty shall be laid on articles exported from any state.

No preference shall be given by any regulation of commerce or revenue to the ports of one state over those of another: nor shall vessels bound to, or from, one state be obliged to enter, clear, or pay duties in another.

No money shall be drawn from the treasury, but in consequence of appropriations made by law; and a regular statement and account of the receipts and expenditures of all public money shall be published from time to time.

No title of nobility shall be granted by the United States; and no person holding any office of profit or trust under them, shall, without the consent of the Congress, accept of any present, emolument, office, or title, of any kind what-ever, from any king, prince, or foreign state.

Congress does <u>not</u> have these powers:

1. Congress cannot send people to jail without a fair trial.

2. Congress cannot tax goods that are shipped between states.

3. Congress cannot spend government money unless it has passed laws that tell Congress how to spend money. For example, Congress can pass a law that tells how much money to spend for the army. Congress must publish information about how it spends government money. This is important because Americans have the right to know how their tax money is used.

4. Congress cannot give any American a special title such as king, queen, or prince. The writers of the Constitution wanted all Americans to be equal before the law. Special titles like king and queen make some people more important than others.

Section 10. Powers Not Given to the States

No state shall enter into any treaty, alliance, or confederation; grant letters of marque and reprisal; coin money; emit bills of credit; make any thing but gold and silver coin a tender in payment of debts; pass any bill of attainder, *ex post facto* law, or law impairing the obligation of contracts, or grant any title of nobility.

No state shall, without the consent of the Congress, lay any imposts or duties on imports or exports, except what may be absolutely necessary for executing its inspection laws: and the net produce of all duties and imposts, laid by any state on imports or exports, shall be for the use of the Treasury of the United States; and all such laws shall be subject to the revision and control of the Congress.

No state shall, without the consent of Congress, lay any duty of tonnage, keep troops, or ships of war in time of peace, enter into any agreement or compact with another state, or with a foreign power, or engage in war, unless actually invaded, or in such imminent danger as will not admit of delay.

The Constitution gives different powers to the **federal** [national government in Washington, D.C.] and state governments. The federal government has all of the powers for working with other countries. States cannot make treaties with other countries. States cannot go to war against other countries. States cannot have their own army and navy. However, states can send soldiers to be part of the National Guard. States cannot make their own money or their own stamps. The federal government makes the same money for all states.

ARTICLE II. THE EXECUTIVE BRANCH

Section 1. President and Vice President

The executive power shall be vested in a President of the United States of America. He shall hold his office during the term of four years, and, together with the Vice President, chosen for the same term, be elected, as follows:

The writers of the Constitution gave the government an executive branch. The job of the executive branch is to carry out the laws that Congress makes. The President is the leader of the executive branch. The writers wanted the President to have less power than a king. They decided to limit his power so he could not take away freedom from Americans the way King George did. They gave the President enough power to be a strong leader. The Vice President helps the President. Both leaders serve four-year terms.

The executive branch helps the government have **checks and balances**. This means that each branch stops the other branches from having too much power. You read in Article 1 that checks and balances allow a President to veto a bill. Only Congress can write and pass laws. But the President can use the veto to stop a bill from becoming a law.

Each state shall appoint, in such manner as the legislature thereof may direct, a number of electors equal to the whole number of Senators and Representatives to which the state may be entitled in the Congress: but no Senator or Representative, or person holding an office of trust or profit under the United States, shall be appointed an elector.

The electors shall meet in their respective states, and vote by ballot for two persons, of whom one at least shall not be an inhabitant of the same state with themselves. And they shall make a list of all the persons voted for, and of the number of votes for each; which list they shall sign and certify, and transmit sealed to the seat of the government of the United States, directed to the President of the Senate. The President of the Senate shall, in the presence of the Senate and House of Representatives, open all the certificates, and the votes shall then be counted. The person having the greatest number of votes shall be the President, if such number be a majority of the whole number of electors appointed; and if there be more than one who have such majority, and have an equal number of votes, then the House of Representatives shall immediately choose by ballot one of them for President; and if no person have a majority, then from the five highest on the list the said House shall in like manner choose the President. But in choosing the President, the votes shall be taken by states, the representation from each state having one vote; a quorum for this purpose shall consist of a member or members from two thirds of the states, and a majority of all the states shall be necessary to a choice. In every case, after the choice of the President, the person having the greatest number of votes of the electors shall be the Vice President. But if there should remain two or more who have equal votes, the Senate shall choose from them by ballot the Vice President.

The Congress may determine the time of choosing the electors, and the day on which they shall give their votes; which day shall be the same throughout the United States.

The Constitution has rules about how to elect the President and Vice President. These rules were changed by the 12th Amendment in 1804.

The Constitution said people should vote for people called **electors**. The number of electors for each state is the same as the number of senators and representatives a state has in Congress. The electors vote for the President and Vice President. The person who wins the most **electoral votes** [votes from electors] becomes the next President. Elections for President are held on a Tuesday in early November.

No person except a natural-born citizen, or a citizen of the United States, at the time of the adoption of this Constitution, shall be eligible to the office of President; neither shall any person be eligible to that office who shall not have attained the age of 35 years, and been 14 years a resident within the United States.

The President must be a person who was born in the United States. He must be at least 35 years old. He must have lived in the United States for at least 14 years. The writers did not say the President must be a man. But all American Presidents have been men.

~~In case of the removal of the President from office, or of his death, resignation, or inability to discharge the powers and duties of the said office, the same shall~~ ~~devolve on the Vice President,~~ and the Congress may by law provide for the case of removal, death, resignation, or inability, both of the President and Vice President, declaring what officer shall then act as President, and such officer shall act accordingly until the disability be removed, or a President shall be elected.

The Vice President becomes the President if the President dies, leaves the job, or cannot work. If the country does not have a Vice President, Congress must decide who will become President.

The President shall, at stated times, receive for his services a compensation, which shall neither be increased nor diminished during the period for which he shall have been elected, and he shall not receive within that period any other emolument from the United States, or any of them.

The President must be paid a salary. Congress decides how much the President will be paid. The writers of the Constitution wanted poor people and rich people to be able to be President. Since the President earns a salary, a poor person would be able to have this job.

George Washington, the first President, was paid $25,000. In 2001, Congress voted to pay President George W. Bush $400,000. Today, most famous baseball players earn much more money than the President.

Before he enter on the execution of his office, he shall take the following oath or affirmation:

"I do solemnly swear (or affirm) that I will faithfully execute the office of President of the United States, and will to the best of my ability, preserve, protect, and defend the Constitution of the United States."

On the day a person becomes President, he must make a promise to the American people. That promise is called the **Presidential Oath**. The President promises to carry out the duties of his new job. He also promises to protect the Constitution and carry out its laws.

Section 2. President's Powers

The President shall be Commander in Chief of the Army and Navy of the United States, and of the militia of the several states, when called into the actual service of the United States; he may require the opinion, in writing, of the principal officer in each of the executive departments, upon any subject relating to the duties of their respective offices, and he shall have power to grant reprieves and pardons for offenses against the United States, except in cases of impeachment.

He shall have power, by and with the advice and consent of the Senate, to make treaties, provided two thirds of the Senators present concur; and he shall nominate, and by and with the advice and consent of the Senate, shall appoint ambassadors, other public ministers and consuls, judges of the Supreme Court, and all other officers of the United States, whose appointments are not herein otherwise provided for, and which shall be established by law: but the Congress may by law vest the appointment of such inferior officers, as they think proper, in the President alone, in the courts of law, or in the heads of departments.

The President shall have power to fill up all vacancies that may happen during the recess of the Senate, by granting commissions which shall expire at the end of their next session.

The President has these important powers:

1. The President is commander-in-chief of the Army, Navy, and National Guard.

2. The President can **pardon** [forgive] people who have done crimes against the federal government. People who are pardoned by the President cannot be put on trial. They cannot be sent to jail.

3. The President can make treaties with other countries. But the Senate must vote to approve these treaties. The President can **appoint** [give jobs to] people to work as ambassadors [representatives] to other countries. The President appoints new judges for the Supreme Court. The Senate must vote to approve the people who are given these jobs. These are more examples of checks and balances in the Constitution. The President can have a **cabinet**, a group of department leaders who work with him. One important executive department is the Department of State. Department leaders are called secretaries.

Section 3. Other Powers

He shall from time to time give to the Congress information of the state of the Union, and recommend to their consideration such measures as he shall judge necessary and expedient; he may, on extraordinary occasions, convene both Houses, or either of them, and in case of disagreement between them, with respect to the time of adjournment, he may adjourn them to such time as he shall think proper; he shall receive ambassadors and other public ministers; he shall take care that the laws be faithfully executed, and shall commission all the officers of the United States.

The President has other jobs that must be done:

1. The President must give a speech to both houses of Congress. Most of the time the President does this in January. The speech is called the **State of the Union address**.

2. The President can ask Congress to meet if there are emergencies that must be worked on.

3. The President can ask Congress to write new laws.

4. The President must meet with ambassadors from other countries. He can decide how the United States will work with other countries.

5. The President must carry out all laws made by Congress.

Section 4. Impeachment

The President, Vice President, and all civil officers of the United States, shall be removed from office on impeachment for, and conviction of, treason, bribery, or other high crimes and misdemeanors.

The President, Vice President and other government leaders can be impeached. They can be impeached for helping enemies of the United States. They can also be impeached for doing crimes.

ARTICLE III. THE JUDICIAL BRANCH

Section 1. Judges

The judicial power of the United States, shall be vested in one Supreme Court, and in such inferior courts as the Congress may from time to time ordain and establish. The judges, both of the Supreme and inferior courts, shall hold their offices during good behavior, and shall, at stated times, receive for their services, a compensation, which shall not be diminished during their continuance in office.

The judicial branch is the third branch of government. The Supreme Court has the power to judge if laws and actions obey the Constitution. It is the highest court in the United States. Congress has the power to make lower courts.

The judges of the Supreme Court can keep their jobs for as long as they live. Lower federal court judges also keep their jobs for as long as they live.

The writers of the Constitution did not want judges to be afraid of Congress or the President when making decisions. Congress or the President might not like their decisions. So the writers gave the judges lifetime jobs so they would make honest decisions and not lose their jobs.

Section 2. Federal Courts

The judicial power shall extend to all cases, in law and equity, arising under this Constitution, the laws of the United States, and treaties made, or which shall be made, under their authority; to all cases affecting ambassadors, other public ministers and consuls; to all cases of admiralty and maritime jurisdiction; to controversies to which the United States shall be a party; to controversies between two or more states, ~~between a state and citizens of another state;~~ between citizens of different states; between citizens of the same state claiming lands under grants of different states, ~~and between a state, or the citizens thereof, and foreign states, citizens or subjects~~.

Federal courts can hear many kinds of cases. Cases may be about the laws of Congress, problems between two states, and other kinds of problems.

The Supreme Court has a very important power. It is the power of **judicial review**. This means the Supreme Court can decide if any law in the nation is **unconstitutional**. An unconstitutional law does not obey the Constitution. Unconstitutional laws must be changed. This is another example of checks and balances. The Supreme Court can force both the states and Congress to change laws that are against the Constitution. It can also force the President to change actions that are against the Constitution.

In all cases affecting ambassadors, other public ministers and consuls, and those in which a state shall be party, the Supreme Court shall have original jurisdiction. In all the other cases before mentioned, the Supreme Court shall have appellate jurisdiction, both as to law and fact, with such exceptions, and under such regulations, as the Congress shall make.

The Supreme Court is sometimes the first court to hear a case. Most of the time the Supreme Court hears cases that were already heard in a lower court. The Supreme Court can change a decision that was made by a lower court. But Supreme Court decisions are final. They cannot be changed by any other court.

The trial of all crimes, except in cases of impeachment, shall be by jury; and such trial shall be held in the state where the said crimes shall have been committed; but when not committed within any state, the trial shall be at such place or places as the Congress may by law have directed.

All people accused of federal crimes can have a jury trial.

The writers of the Constitution believed that every person must have the right to a fair jury trial.

Section 3. Treason

Treason against the United States, shall consist only in levying war against them, or in adhering to their enemies, giving them aid and comfort. No person shall be convicted of treason unless on the testimony of two witnesses to the same overt act, or on confession in open court.

The Congress shall have power to declare the punishment of treason, but no attainder of treason shall work corruption of blood, or forfeiture except during the life of the person attainted.

Treason means helping the enemies of the United States. A court can find a person guilty of treason only if two people tell a judge that they saw the same act of treason. Guilty people may also tell a judge that they did acts of treason.

Congress can make laws to punish people who are guilty of treason. The guilty person's family and friends cannot be punished.

ARTICLE IV. RELATIONS BETWEEN STATES

Section 1. Laws

Full faith and credit shall be given in each state to the public acts, records, and judicial proceedings of every other state. And the Congress may by general laws prescribe the manner in which such acts, records, and proceedings shall be proved, and the effect thereof.

Every state must respect the laws of every other state. For example, each state has its own marriage laws. People can get married in one state and then move to another state. The new state must accept that the people are married.

Section 2. Citizens

The citizens of each state shall be entitled to all privileges and immunities of citizens in the several states.

People from one state can visit other states. They have the same rights as the citizens of the state.

A person charged in any state with treason, felony, or other crimes, who shall flee from justice, and be found in another state, shall, on demand of the executive authority of the state from which he fled, be delivered up, to be removed to the state having jurisdiction of the crime.

People may do crimes and escape to other states. When those people are found, they must be returned to the state they came from.

~~No person held to service or labor in one state, under the laws thereof, escaping into another, shall, in consequence of any laws or regulation therein, be discharged from such service or labor, but shall be delivered up on claim of the party to whom such service or labor may be due.~~

Section 3. States and Territories

New states may be admitted by the Congress into this Union; but no new state shall be formed or erected within the jurisdiction of any other state; nor any state be formed by the junction of two or more states, or parts of states, without the consent of the legislatures of the states concerned, as well as of the Congress.

The Congress shall have power to dispose of and make all needful rules and regulations respecting the territory or other property belonging to the United States; and nothing in this Constitution shall be so construed as to prejudice any claims of the United States, or of any particular state.

Congress has the power to allow new states to become part of the United Stages. Since 1787, 37 states have become part of the United States.

The United States also owns public land and territories such as the island of Guam. Only Congress can make rules about selling or controlling public land and territories.

Section 4. Protecting the States

The United States shall guarantee to every state in this Union a republican form of government, and shall protect each of them against invasion; and on application of the legislature, or of the executive (when the legislature cannot be convened) against domestic violence.

Every state of the United States must have a government that has three branches. It must have a lawmaking branch, an executive branch, and a judicial branch. A state cannot have a king as a leader. If fighting starts in a state, the National Guard can be called in to end the fighting in the state.

ARTICLE V. ADDING AMENDMENTS

The Congress, whenever two thirds of both Houses shall deem it necessary, shall propose amendments to this Constitution, or, on the application of the legislatures of two thirds of the several states, shall call a convention for proposing amendments, which, in either case, shall be valid to all intents and purposes, as part of this Constitution, when ratified by the legislatures of three fourths of the several states, or by conventions in three fourths thereof, as the one or the other mode of ratification may be proposed by the Congress; provided that no amendment which may be made prior to the year 1808 shall in any manner affect the first and fourth clauses in the ninth section of the first article; and that no state, without its consent, shall be deprived of its equal suffrage in the Senate.

Amendments, or new laws, can be added to the Constitution. This article of the Constitution tells how new amendments can be added. It is difficult to add new amendments. Since 1787, only 27 amendments have been added to the Constitution.

ARTICLE VI. THE SUPREME LAW OF THE LAND

All debts contracted and engagements entered into, before the adoption of this Constitution, shall be as valid against the United States, under this Constitution, as under the Confederation.

The United States borrowed money to pay for the American Revolution. It also borrowed money after the war. The writers of the Constitution decided that the United States must repay all of the money it had borrowed. Other nations would trust the United States because it paid its debts.

This Constitution, and the laws of the United States which shall be made in pursuance thereof; and all treaties made, or which shall be made, under the authority of the United States, shall be the supreme law of the land; and the judges, in every state, shall be bound thereby, anything in the constitution or laws of any state to the contrary notwithstanding.

The Senators and Representatives before mentioned, and the members of the several state legislatures, and all executive and judicial officers, both of the United States and of the several states, shall be bound, by oath or affirmation, to support this Constitution; but no religious test shall ever be required as a qualification to any office or public trust under the United States.

The Constitution is the highest law in the land. All the laws of Congress and all state laws must agree with the Constitution.

All members of Congress must take an oath and promise to obey the Constitution. All members of state governments must take the same oath. Members of the executive and judicial branches must also make the same promise.

Freedom of religion is important in the United States. People never have to be part of a religious group to get a government job.

ARTICLE VII. RATIFICATION

The ratification of the conventions of nine states, shall be sufficient for the establishment of this Constitution between the states so ratifying the same.

Done in convention by the unanimous consent of the states present the 17th day of September in the year of our Lord 1787 and of the independence of the United States of America the 12th. IN WITNESS whereof we have hereunto subscribed our names,

The Constitution will become the nation's law when nine states **ratify** [approve] it. Each state must hold a special meeting to ratify the Constitution.

The Constitution was signed by leaders from 12 states at the end of the Constitutional Convention. It was signed on September 17, 1787. Here are the names of the leaders who signed and the states they came from:

George Washington
President and deputy from Virginia
attest: William Jackson, Secretary

New Hampshire
John Langdon
Nicholas Gilman

Massachusetts
Nathaniel Gorham
Rufus King

Connecticut
William Samuel Johnson
Roger Sherman

New York
Alexander Hamilton

New Jersey
William Livingston
David Brearley
William Paterson
Jonathan Dayton

Pennsylvania
Benjamin Franklin
Thomas Mifflin
Robert Morris
George Clymer
Thomas FitzSimons
Jared Ingersoll
James Wilson
Gouverneur Morris

Delaware
George Read
Gunning Bedford, Jr.
John Dickinson
Richard Bassett
Jacob Broom

Maryland
James McHenry

Daniel of St. Thomas Jenifer
Daniel Carroll

Virginia
John Blair
James Madison, Jr.

North Carolina
William Blount
Richard Dobbs Spaight
Hugh Williamson

South Carolina
John Rutledge
Charles Cotesworth Pinckney
Charles Pinckney
Pierce Butler

Georgia
William Few
Abraham Baldwin

The Constitution was ratified in 1788. In 1789 Congress met for the first time. That year George Washington became the first President of the United States.

AMENDMENTS

In 1791 the first ten amendments became part of the Constitution. These amendments are called the Bill of Rights. The Bill of Rights protects the freedom of all Americans.

AMENDMENT I. Freedom of Religion, Speech, Press, Assembly, and Petition

Congress shall make no law respecting an establishment of religion, or prohibiting the free exercise thereof; or abridging the freedom of speech, or of the press; or the right of the people peaceably to assemble, and to petition the government for a redress of grievances.

The First Amendment is very important because it protects five kinds of freedom. It protects freedom of religion. It protects freedom of speech. This allows people to speak against the government and not be sent to jail. This amendment protects freedom of the press. This allows people to write stories that may be against the government in books and newspapers. The First Amendment protects the right to **assemble** [to stand with a large group of people and protest peacefully against government actions]. It also protects your right to **petition** [ask the government to correct problems].

Freedom of religion was very important to the people who wrote the Constitution. They remembered that the Pilgrims and other groups first came to America because they did not want to pray in the Church of England. The writers of the Constitution wanted America to be different than England. They believed the government should not force people to belong to any religion. So the First Amendment also says that Congress cannot write laws that make one religion the main religion of the nation. The First Amendment also says there must be **separation of church and state**. This means that religion must be completely separate from the government. Tax money cannot be used to build churches or other religious buildings. Tax money cannot be used to pay church leaders. Classes in public schools cannot teach about religion.

AMENDMENT II. The Right to Bear Arms

A well regulated militia, being necessary to the security of a free state, the right of the people to keep and bear arms shall not be infringed.

Every state needs soldiers to protect its people. Today soldiers of the National Guard protect people in the United States. The government cannot stop people from owning guns. The federal and state governments can pass laws to control how guns are sold.

AMENDMENT III. The Housing of Soldiers

No soldier shall, in time of peace, be quartered in any house, without the consent of the owner, nor in time of war, but in a manner to be prescribed by law.

Before the American Revolution, the British forced Americans to have British soldiers in their homes. The writers did not want Americans to have this problem again. So this amendment says people cannot be forced to have soldiers eat and sleep in their homes when the United States has peace with other countries. During a war, Congress can pass a law that says soldiers must be allowed to sleep in the homes of Americans.

AMENDMENT IV. Search and Arrest

The right of the people to be secure in their persons, houses, papers, and effects, against unreasonable searches and seizures, shall not be violated, and no warrants shall issue, but upon probable cause, supported by oath or affirmation, and particularly describing the place to be searched, and the persons or things to be seized.

People have the right to be safe in their own homes. The police cannot search a person's home without a **warrant** [a search paper from a judge]. Judges must have very good reasons to give the police search warrants.

AMENDMENT V. The Rights of Accused Persons

No person shall be held to answer for a capital, or otherwise infamous crime, unless on a presentment or indictment of a grand jury, except in cases arising in the land or naval forces, or in the militia, when in actual service, in time of war or public danger; nor shall any person be subject for the same offenses to be twice put in jeopardy of life or limb; nor shall be compelled in any criminal case to be a witness against himself, nor be deprived of life, liberty, or property, without due process of law; nor shall private property be taken for public use without just compensation.

The Fifth Amendment protects people who may have done crimes. A **grand jury**, a jury of about 25 people, must listen to information about the accused person. Then the grand jury decides if the person should have a jury trial because the person may be guilty. The grand jury may decide that the accused person does not need a trial because there is not enough information to prove the person may be guilty. Then the accused person is allowed to remain free.

Accused people cannot be forced to speak against themselves during a trial. Instead, during a trial they can say, "I take the Fifth Amendment." Every accused person has the right to **due process** [fair treatment that obeys the law].

AMENDMENT VI. The Right to a Fair Trial

In all criminal prosecutions, the accused shall enjoy the right to a speedy and public trial, by an impartial jury of the state and district wherein the crime shall have been committed, which district shall have been previously ascertained by law, and to be informed of the nature and cause of the accusation; to be confronted with the witnesses against him; to have compulsory process for obtaining witnesses in his favor; and to have the assistance of counsel for his defense.

The writers of the Constitution wanted the United States to be different from Great Britain. In Great Britain, accused people sometimes stayed in jail for years before they had a trial. Sometimes the trials were held secretly. The writers wanted to be fair to accused people. In the United States, every person who is accused of a crime has the right to a fair jury. The trials cannot be held secretly. Every accused person also has the right to have a lawyer help with the trial. A person may not have enough money to pay for a lawyer. Then a government lawyer will help the accused person both before and during the trial.

AMENDMENT VII. Civil Cases

In suits at common law, where the value in controversy shall exceed twenty dollars, the right of trial by jury shall be preserved, and no fact tried by a jury, shall be otherwise re-examined in any court of the United States, than according to the rules of the common law.

This amendment says people have the right to a jury trial in **civil cases**. Civil cases are not about crimes. They are often about money, property, or divorce. Today people can have jury trials for civil cases in both federal and state courts.

AMENDMENT VIII. Bail and Punishment

Excessive bail shall not be required, nor excessive fines imposed, nor cruel and unusual punishments inflicted.

People who are accused of crimes can often stay out of jail until their trial if they pay **bail** money. Bail is money that an accused person gives the court. When people pay bail, they promise to be in court for their trial. They promise not to run away. The bail money is returned when accused people go to their trials. People who do not have enough money to pay bail must wait in jail until their trial. This amendment helps accused people because it says courts cannot ask people to pay unfair amounts of bail money.

This amendment also protects people who have been found guilty during their trial. Guilty people cannot be punished in ways that are not fair and cruel. For example, a person may be found guilty of stealing a small amount of money. It would not be fair to keep this person in jail for many years.

AMENDMENT IX. Other Rights

The enumeration in the Constitution, of certain rights, shall not be construed to deny or disparage others retained by the people.

The Constitution explains certain rights like freedom of religion and speech. But people have many other rights such as the right to go to school or to work. Many rights are not explained in the Constitution. The government must protect all rights that people have even if they are not in the Constitution.

AMENDMENT X. Powers Belonging to States

The powers not delegated to the United States by the Constitution, nor prohibited by it to the states, are reserved to the states respectively, or to the people.

This is the last amendment in the Bill of Rights. The writers of the Constitution wanted to be sure the federal government would not become too powerful. Many people feared that the states would not have enough power. This amendment says that powers not given to the federal government belong to state governments and their people. For example, the Constitution did not give the federal government the power to make laws about marriage and divorce. So the states have the power to make marriage and divorce laws.

AMENDMENT XI. Cases Against States (1795)

The judicial power of the United States shall not be construed to extend to any suit in law or equity, commenced or prosecuted against one of the United States by citizens of any state, or by citizens or subjects of any foreign state.

A person from one state cannot have a trial against another state in a federal court. A person from a different country cannot do this either.

AMENDMENT XII. Election of the President and Vice President (1804)

The electors shall meet in their respective states and vote by ballot for President and Vice President, one of whom, at least, shall not be an inhabitant of the same state with themselves; they shall name in their ballots the person voted for as President, and in distinct ballots the person voted for as Vice President, and they shall make distinct lists of all persons voted for as President, and of all persons voted for as Vice President, and of the number of votes for each, which lists they shall sign and certify, and transmit sealed to the seat of the government of the United States, directed to the President of the Senate; the President of the Senate shall, in the presence of the Senate and House of Representatives, open all the certificates and the votes shall then be counted. The person having the greatest number of votes for President shall be the President, if such number be a majority of the whole number of electors appointed; and if no person have such majority, then from the persons having the highest numbers, not exceeding three on the list of those voted for as President, the House of Representatives shall choose immediately, by ballot, the President. But in choosing the President, the votes shall be taken by states, the representation from each state having one vote; a quorum for this purpose shall consist of a member or members from two-thirds of the states, and a majority of all the states shall be necessary to a choice. ~~And if the House of Representatives shall not choose a President whenever the right of choice shall devolve upon them, before the fourth day of March next following, then the Vice President shall act as President, as in the case of the death or other constitutional disability of the President.~~ The person having the greatest number of votes as Vice President, shall be the Vice President, if such number be a majority of the whole number of electors appointed, and if no person have a majority, then from the two highest numbers on the list, the Senate shall choose the Vice President; a quorum for the purpose shall consist of two-thirds of the whole number of Senators, and a majority of the whole number shall be necessary to a choice. But no person constitutionally ineligible to the office of President shall be eligible to that of Vice President of the United States.

Article II of the Constitution changed the way Americans elect a President. Until 1800, people voted for electors. The electors then voted for the President. They had two **candidates** [people who want to be elected] to vote for. The candidate who received the most electoral votes became President. The other candidate became the Vice President. In 1800, both Thomas Jefferson and Aaron Burr wanted to be President. Both men received the same

number of votes. So members of the House of Representatives had to vote for one of the men to be President. The House chose Jefferson but many people were unhappy about the election.

The Twelfth Amendment was written to improve the way Americans choose a President. The new amendment said electors must vote separately for President and Vice President. The candidate for President must win the **majority** [more than half] of electoral votes to become President. The candidate for Vice President must also win the majority of votes. The House of Representatives votes for a President if a candidate does not receive a majority of electoral votes. The Senate elects the Vice President if no candidate receives a majority of votes.

AMENDMENT XIII. Slavery (1865)

Section 1. Neither slavery nor involuntary servitude, except as a punishment for a crime whereof the party shall have been duly convicted, shall exist within the United States, or any place subject to their jurisdiction.

Section 2. Congress shall have power to enforce this article by appropriate legislation.

This amendment ended slavery in the United States. Congress has the power to carry out this amendment.

AMENDMENT XIV. Rights of Citizens (1868)

Section 1. All persons born or naturalized in the United States, and subject to the jurisdiction thereof, are citizens of the United States and of the state wherein they reside. No state shall make or enforce any law which shall abridge the privileges or immunities of citizens of the United States; nor shall any state deprive any person of life, liberty, or property, without due process of law; nor deny to any person within its jurisdiction the equal protection of the laws.

Section 2. Representatives shall be apportioned among the several states according to their respective numbers, counting the whole number of persons in each state, excluding Indians not taxed. But when the right to vote at any election for the choice of electors for President and Vice President of the United States, representatives in Congress, the executive and judicial officers of a state, or the members of the legislature thereof, is denied to any of the male inhabitants of such state, being 21 years of age, and citizens of the United States, or in anyway abridged, except for participation in rebellion or other crime, the basis of representation therein shall be reduced in the proportion which the number of such male citizens shall bear to the whole number of male citizens 21 years of age in such state.

Section 3. No person shall be a Senator or Representative in Congress, or elector of President and Vice President, or hold any office, civil or military, under the United States, or under any state, who, having previously taken an oath, as a member of Congress, or as an officer of the United States, or as a member of any state legislature, or as an executive or judicial officer of any state, to support the Constitution of the United States, shall

have engaged in insurrection or rebellion against the same, or given aid or comfort to the enemies thereof. But Congress may, by a vote of two-thirds of each house, remove such disability.

Section 4. The validity of the public debt of the United States, authorized by law, including debts incurred for payment of pensions and bounties for services in suppressing insurrection or rebellion, shall not be questioned. But neither the United States nor any state shall assume or pay any debt or obligation incurred in aid of insurrection or rebellion against the United States, or any claim for the loss or emancipation of any slave; but all such debts, obligations and claims shall be held illegal and void.

The Fourteenth Amendment is one of the most important. It has these laws:

1. All people who are born in the United States are citizens. People from other nations can follow certain laws to become citizens. Before this amendment was written, African Americans could not be citizens. The Fourteenth Amendment said African Americans were citizens of both their state and the United States. All people must have equal rights. States must protect the rights of all people.

2. The number of members a state sends to the House of Representatives depends on the state's population. African Americans must be counted as part of a state's population. States must allow all men who are more than 21 years old to vote.

3. People who have worked against the United States cannot be in Congress.

They cannot be part of the federal government. This law punished people who fought for the South during the Civil War.

4. The United States borrowed a lot of money to pay for the Civil War. The government must repay the money.

5. Congress can make laws to carry out the Fourteenth Amendment.

Section 5. The Congress shall have power to enforce, by appropriate legislation, the provisions of this article.

AMENDMENT XV. Right to Vote (1870)

Section 1. The right of citizens of the United States to vote shall not be denied or abridged by the United States or by any state on account of race, color, or previous condition of servitude.

Section 2. The Congress shall have power to enforce this article by appropriate legislation.

All citizens who are men can vote. This amendment gave African Americans the right to vote. Congress can make laws to carry out this amendment.

AMENDMENT XVI. Income Tax (1913)

The Congress shall have power to lay and collect taxes on incomes, from whatever source derived, without apportionment among the several states, and without regard to any census or enumeration.

Congress can write laws about **income taxes** and collect income taxes. Income tax is a tax on the money people earn.

AMENDMENT XVII. Election of Senators (1913)

The Senate of the United States shall be composed of two Senators from each state, elected by the people thereof, for six years; and each Senator shall have one vote. The electors in each state shall have the qualifications requisite for electors of the most numerous branch of the state legislatures.

When vacancies happen in the representation of any state in the Senate, the executive authority of such state shall issue writs of election to fill such vacancies: *Provided*, That the legislature of any state may empower the executive thereof to make temporary appointments until the people fill the vacancies by election as the legislature may direct.

This amendment shall not be so construed as to effect the election or term of any Senator chosen before it becomes valid as part of the Constitution.

This amendment changed the way Americans elect United States senators. The people of each state vote for senators in November elections. They vote for senators the same way they vote for members of the House of Representatives. This method continues to be the one that is used today.

AMENDMENT XVIII. Prohibition of Liquor (1919)

Section 1. After one year from the ratification of this article the manufacture, sale, or transportation of intoxicating liquors within, the importation thereof into, or the exportation thereof from the United States and all territory subject to

~~the jurisdiction thereof for beverage purposes is hereby prohibited.~~

~~Section 2. The Congress and the several states shall have concurrent power to enforce this article by appropriate legislation.~~

~~Section 3. This article shall be inoperative unless it shall have been ratified as an amendment to the Constitution by the legislatures of the several states, as provided in the Constitution, within seven years from the date of the submission hereof to the states by the Congress.~~

This amendment said that **liquor** [drinks like wine, beer, and whiskey] could not be made, bought, or sold in the United States. Millions of people did not agree with this law. A lot of liquor was bought and sold in ways that were against the law.

AMENDMENT XIX. Woman Suffrage (1920)

The right of citizens of the United States to vote shall not be denied or abridged by the United States or by any state on account of sex.

Congress shall have power to enforce this article by appropriate legislation.

All women who are citizens have the right to vote in all elections. Congress has the power to pass laws to carry out this amendment.

AMENDMENT XX. Lame Duck Amendment (1933)

Section 1. The terms of the President and Vice President shall end at noon on the 20th day of January, and the terms of Senators and Representatives at noon on the third day of January, of the years in which such terms would have ended if this article had not been ratified; and the terms of their successors shall then begin.

Section 2. The Congress shall assemble at least once in every year, and such meeting shall begin at noon on the third day of January, unless they shall by law appoint a different day.

Section 3. If, at the time fixed for the beginning of the term of the President, the President elect shall have died, the Vice President elect shall become President. If a President shall not have been chosen before the time fixed for the beginning of his term, or if the President elect shall have failed to qualify, then the Vice President elect shall act as President until a President shall have qualified; and the Congress may by law provide for the case wherein neither a President elect nor a Vice President elect shall have qualified, declaring who shall then act as President, or the manner in which one who is to act shall be selected, and such person shall act accordingly until a President or Vice President shall have qualified.

Section 4. The Congress may by law provide for the case of the death of any of the persons from whom the House of Representatives may choose a President whenever the right of choice shall have devolved upon them, and for the case of the death of any of the persons from whom the Senate may choose a Vice President whenever the right of choice shall have devolved upon them.

Section 5. Sections 1 and 2 shall take effect on the 15th day of October following the ratification of this article.

Section 6. This article shall be inoperative unless it shall have been ratified as an amendment to the Constitution by the legislatures of three-fourths of the several states within seven years from the date of its submission.

Each new President and Vice President begin their term on January 20. The terms for senators and members of the House begin on January 3. Before this amendment was passed, people who won elections in November did not begin their terms until March.

Congress must meet at least once a year. The meetings should begin on January 3 at noon.

If the President dies, the Vice President becomes the next President.

AMENDMENT XXI. Repeal of the Eighteenth Amendment (1933)

Section 1. The Eighteenth article of amendment to the Constitution of the United States is hereby repealed.

Section 2. The transportation or importation into any state, territory, or possession of the United States for delivery or use therein of intoxicating liquors, in violation of the laws thereof, is hereby prohibited.

Section 3. This article shall be inoperative unless it shall have been ratified as an amendment to the Constitution by conventions in the several states, as provided in the Constitution,

within seven years from the date of the submission hereof to the states by the Congress.

The Eighteenth Amendment on prohibition is no longer a law of the United States. States can pass their own laws about buying and selling liquor.

AMENDMENT XXII. Terms of the Presidency (1951)

Section 1. No person shall be elected to the office of the President more than twice, and no person who has held the office of President, or acted as President, for more than two years of a term to which some other person was elected President shall be elected to the office of the President more than once. But this article shall not apply to any person holding the office of President when this article was proposed by the Congress, and shall not prevent any person who may be holding the office of President, or acting as President, during the term within which this article becomes operative from holding the office of President or acting as President during the remainder of such term.

Section 2. This article shall be inoperative unless it shall have been ratified as an amendment to the Constitution by the legislatures of three fourths of the several States within seven years from the date of its submission to the States by Congress.

A person cannot be elected President for more than two terms. A person cannot be President for more than ten years.

George Washington was President for two terms. Every President served only one or two terms until Franklin D. Roosevelt became President. He was elected to four terms. Many people feared that a President could become too powerful if he served for so many years. This amendment was added to the Constitution to prevent that problem.

AMENDMENT XXIII. Voting in the District of Columbia (1961)

Section 1. The district constituting the seat of government of the United States shall appoint in such manner as the Congress may direct: A number of electors of President and Vice President equal to the whole number of Senators and Representatives in Congress to which the district would be entitled if it were a state, but in no event more than the least populous state; they shall be in addition to those appointed by the states, but they shall be considered, for the purposes of the election of the President and Vice President, to be electors appointed by a state; and they shall meet in the district and perform such duties as provided by the Twelfth article of amendment.

This amendment allows the citizens of Washington, D.C., to vote in elections for President. Washington, D.C., has three electoral votes. Congress has the power to write laws to carry out this amendment.

Washington, D.C., the capital of the United States, is in the District of Columbia. The capital city is between the states of Maryland and Virginia but it is not part of any state. People who lived in the nation's capital city were never allowed to vote in elections for President. This amendment changed that problem. Washington, D.C., has about the same population as some of the smallest states. So the capital city has three electoral votes that is the same number of votes given to states with the smallest populations.

The people of Washington D.C., cannot vote for members of Congress. Many Americans believe it is not fair that citizens of the capital are not represented in Congress. They hope that some day another amendment will be added to the Constitution to solve this problem.

Section 2. The Congress shall have power to enforce this article by appropriate legislation.

AMENDMENT XXIV. Poll Taxes (1964)

Section 1. The right of citizens of the United States to vote in any primary or other election for President or Vice President, for electors for President or Vice President, or for Senator or Representative in Congress, shall not be denied or abridged by the United States or any state by reason of failure to pay any poll tax or other tax.

Section 2. The Congress shall have the power to enforce this article by appropriate legislation.

A **poll tax** is a tax that people had to pay in order to vote. After 1889 many states had poll taxes. Poll taxes made it difficult for poor African Americans to vote. This amendment said people could not lose their right to vote in national elections because they could not pay a poll tax. Congress has the power to make laws to carry out this amendment. Today all poll taxes are unconstitutional.

AMENDMENT XXV. Presidential Succession (1967)

Section 1. In case of the removal of the President from office or his death or resignation, the Vice President shall become President.

Section 2. Whenever there is a vacancy in the office of the Vice President, the President shall nominate a Vice President who shall take office upon confirmation by a majority vote of both houses of Congress.

Section 3. Whenever the President transmits to the president *pro tempore* of the Senate and the Speaker of the House of Representatives his written declaration that he is unable to discharge the powers and duties of his office, and until he transmits to them a written declaration to the contrary, such powers and duties shall be discharged by the Vice President as Acting President.

Section 4. Whenever the Vice President and a majority of either the principal officers of the executive departments or of such other body as Congress may by law provide, transmit to the President pro tempore of the Senate and the Speaker of the House of Representatives their written declaration that the President is unable to discharge the powers and duties of his office, the Vice President shall immediately assume the powers and duties of the office as Acting President.

Thereafter, when the President transmits to the President pro tempore of the Senate and the Speaker of the House of Representatives his written declaration that no inability exists, he shall resume the powers and duties of his office unless the Vice President and a majority of either the principal officers of the executive department or of such other body as Congress may by law provide, transmit within four days to the President pro tempore of the Senate and the Speaker of the House of Representatives their written declaration that the President is unable to discharge the powers and duties of his office. Thereupon Congress shall decide the issue, assembling within 48 hours for that purpose if not in session. If the Congress, within 21 days after receipt of the latter written declaration, or, if Congress is not in session, within 21 days after Congress is required to assemble, determines by two-thirds vote of both houses that the President is unable to discharge the powers and duties of his office, the Vice President shall continue to discharge the same as Acting President; otherwise, the President shall resume the powers and duties of his office.

This amendment tries to solve the problem of what to do if the President dies or cannot work. If the President dies or **resigns** [leaves his job], then the Vice President becomes President.

If the Vice President dies or leaves his job, the nation needs a new Vice President. The President can choose a person to be Vice President. Both houses of Congress must vote to approve the person chosen for Vice President.

If a President is sick or not able to do his job, the Vice President will do the job until the President can work again. Once the President is able to work, the Vice President will return to his job of being Vice President.

AMENDMENT XXVI. Voting Age of 18 (1971)

Section 1. The right of citizens of the United States, who are 18 years of age or older, to vote shall not be denied or abridged by the United States or by any state on account of age.

Section 2. The Congress shall have power to enforce this article by appropriate legislation.

All citizens who are at least 18 years old can vote in state and national elections. Congress can make laws to carry out this amendment.

In 1787, only white men could vote. As time passed, new amendments allowed more and more people to vote. Today all citizens who are at least eighteen years old can vote.

AMENDMENT XXVII. Congressional Pay (1992)

No law varying the compensation for the services of the Senators and Representatives shall take effect, until an election of Representatives shall have intervened.

This amendment allows Congress to raise salaries for members of the House and Senate. However, this amendment was written so that members of Congress cannot pay themselves more money. But the higher salaries will be paid after the next election for Senators and Representatives. The new members of Congress will receive the higher salaries. In 2004, the salary for members of Congress was $158,100.

The Fifty States

Alabama

Date of Statehood 1819,
  order 22nd
Area in Square Miles 51,718, **rank** 29th
Population 4,500,752, **rank** 23rd

State Symbols
State tree Southern pine
State flower Camellia
State bird Yellowhammer

Alaska

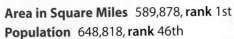

Date of Statehood 1959,
  order 49th
Area in Square Miles 589,878, **rank** 1st
Population 648,818, **rank** 46th

State Symbols
State tree Sitka spruce
State flower Forget-me-not
State bird Willow ptarmigan

Arizona

Date of Statehood 1912,
  order 48th
Area in Square Miles 114,007, **rank** 6th
Population 5,580,811, **rank** 18th

State Symbols
State tree Paloverde
State flower Saguaro cactus
  blossom
State bird Cactus wren

Arkansas

Date of Statehood 1836,
  order 25th
Area in Square Miles 53,183, **rank** 27th
Population 2,725,714, **rank** 32nd

State Symbols
State tree Pine tree
State flower Apple blossom
State bird Mockingbird

California

Date of Statehood 1850,
  order 31st
Area in Square Miles 158,648, **rank** 3rd
Population 35,484,453, **rank** 1st

State Symbols
State tree California redwood
State flower Golden poppy
State bird California valley quail

Colorado

Date of Statehood 1876,
  order 38th
Area in Square Miles 104,091, **rank** 8th
Population 4,550,688, **rank** 22nd

State Symbols
State tree Blue spruce
State flower Rocky Mountain
  columbine
State bird Lark bunting

Population estimates are based on 2003 information from the United States Census Bureau.

Connecticut

Date of Statehood 1788,
    order 5th
Area in Square Miles 5,006, **rank** 48th
Population 3,483,372, **rank** 29th

State Symbols

State tree White oak
State flower Mountain laurel
State bird Robin

Georgia

Date of Statehood 1788,
    order 4th
Area in Square Miles 58,930, **rank** 21st
Population 8,684,715, **rank** 9th

State Symbols

State tree Live oak
State flower Cherokee rose
State bird Brown thrasher

Delaware

Date of Statehood 1787,
    order 1st
Area in Square Miles 2,026, **rank** 49th
Population 817,491, **rank** 45th

State Symbols

State tree American holly
State flower Peach blossom
State bird Blue hen chicken

Hawaii

Date of Statehood 1959,
    order 50th
Area in Square Miles 6,459, **rank** 47th
Population 1,257,608, **rank** 42nd

State Symbols

State tree Kukui
State flower Yellow hibiscus
State bird Nene (Hawaiian goose)

Florida

Date of Statehood 1845,
    order 27th
Area in Square Miles 58,681, **rank** 22nd
Population 17,019,068, **rank** 4th

State Symbols
State tree Sabal palmetto palm
State flower Orange blossom
State bird Mockingbird

Idaho

Date of Statehood 1890,
    order 43rd
Area in Square Miles 83,574, **rank** 13th
Population 1,366,332, **rank** 39th

State Symbols
State tree White pine
State flower Syringa
State bird Mountain bluebird

Illinois

Date of Statehood 1818,
    order 21st
Area in Square Miles 56,343, **rank** 24th
Population 12,653,544, **rank** 5th

State Symbols
State tree White oak
State flower Native violet
State bird Cardinal

Kansas

Date of Statehood 1861,
    order 34th
Area in Square Miles 82,282, **rank** 14th
Population 2,723,507, **rank** 33rd

State Symbols
State tree Cottonwood
State flower Sunflower
State bird Western meadowlark

Indiana

Date of Statehood 1816,
    order 19th
Area in Square Miles 36,185, **rank** 38th
Population 6,195,643, **rank** 14th

State Symbols
State tree Tulip tree
State flower Peony
State bird Cardinal

Kentucky

Date of Statehood 1792,
    order 15th
Area in Square Miles 40,395, **rank** 37th
Population 4,117,827, **rank** 26th

State Symbols
State tree Kentucky coffee tree
State flower Goldenrod
State bird Kentucky cardinal

Iowa

Date of Statehood 1846,
    order 29th
Area in Square Miles 56,276, **rank** 25th
Population 2,944,062, **rank** 30th

State Symbols
State tree Oak
State flower Wild rose
State bird Eastern goldfinch

Louisiana

Date of Statehood 1812,
    order 18th
Area in Square Miles 47,752, **rank** 31st
Population 4,496,334, **rank** 24th

State Symbols
State tree Bald cypress
State flower Magnolia
State bird Brown pelican

Maine

Date of Statehood 1820,
    order 23rd
Area in Square Miles 33,128, **rank** 39th
Population 1,305,728, **rank** 40th

State Symbols

State tree White pine
State flower White pine cone
    & tassel
State bird Chickadee

Michigan

Date of Statehood 1837,
    order 26th
Area in Square Miles 58,513, **rank** 23rd
Population 10,079,985, **rank** 8th

State Symbols

State tree White pine
State flower Apple blossom
State bird Robin

Maryland

Date of Statehood 1788,
    order 7th
Area in Square Miles 10,455, **rank** 42nd
Population 5,508,909, **rank** 19th

State Symbols

State tree White oak
State flower Black-eyed Susan
State bird Baltimore oriole

Minnesota

Date of Statehood 1858,
    order 32nd
Area in Square Miles 84,397, **rank** 12th
Population 5,059,375, **rank** 21st

State Symbols

State tree Norway pine
State flower Pink and white lady's
    slipper
State bird Common loon

Massachusetts

Date of Statehood 1788,
    order 6th
Area in Square Miles 8,257, **rank** 45th
Population 6,433,422, **rank** 13th

State Symbols

State tree American elm
State flower Mayflower
    (trailing arbutus)
State bird Chickadee

Mississippi

Date of Statehood 1817,
    order 20th
Area in Square Miles 47,716, **rank** 32nd
Population 2,881,281, **rank** 31st

State Symbols

State tree Magnolia
State flower Magnolia
State bird Mockingbird

Missouri

Date of Statehood 1821,
   order 24th
Area in Square Miles 69,686, **rank** 19th
Population 5,704,484, **rank** 17th

State Symbols
State tree Flowering dogwood
State flower Hawthorn
State bird Bluebird

Nevada

Date of Statehood 1864,
   order 36th
Area in Square Miles 110,561, **rank** 7th
Population 2,241,154, **rank** 35th

State Symbols
State tree Single-leaf piñon &
   bristlecone pine
State flower Sagebrush
State bird Mountain bluebird

Montana

Date of Statehood 1889,
   order 41st
Area in Square Miles 147,047, **rank** 4th
Population 917,621, **rank** 44th

State Symbols
State tree Ponderosa pine
State flower Bitterroot
State bird Western meadowlark

New Hampshire

Date of Statehood 1788,
   order 9th
Area in Square Miles 9,283, **rank** 44th
Population 1,287,687, **rank** 41st

State Symbols
State tree White birch
State flower Purple lilac
State bird Purple finch

Nebraska

Date of Statehood 1867,
   order 37th
Area in Square Miles 77,359, **rank** 15th
Population 1,739,291, **rank** 38th

State Symbols
State tree Cottonwood
State flower Goldenrod
State bird Western meadowlark

New Jersey

Date of Statehood 1787,
   order 3rd
Area in Square Miles 7,790, **rank** 46th
Population 8,638,396, **rank** 10th

State Symbols
State tree Red oak
State flower Purple violet
State bird Eastern goldfinch

New Mexico

Date of Statehood 1912,
   order 47th
Area in Square Miles 121,593, **rank** 5th
Population 1,874,614, **rank** 36th

State Symbols
State tree Piñon
State flower Yucca
State bird Roadrunner

North Dakota

Date of Statehood 1889,
   order 39th
Area in Square Miles 70,704, **rank** 17th
Population 633,837, **rank** 48th

State Symbols
State tree American elm
State flower Wild prairie rose
State bird Western meadowlark

New York

Date of Statehood 1788,
   order 11th
Area in Square Miles 49,112, **rank** 30th
Population 19,190,115, **rank** 3rd

State Symbols
State tree Sugar maple
State flower Rose
State bird Bluebird

Ohio

Date of Statehood 1803,
   order 17th
Area in Square Miles 41,328, **rank** 35th
Population 11,435,798, **rank** 7th

State Symbols
State tree Buckeye
State flower Scarlet carnation
State bird Cardinal

North Carolina

Date of Statehood 1789,
   order 12th
Area in Square Miles 52,672, **rank** 28th
Population 8,407,248, **rank** 11th

State Symbols
State tree Pine
State flower Flowering dogwood
State bird Cardinal

Oklahoma

Date of Statehood 1907,
   order 46th
Area in Square Miles 69,919, **rank** 18th
Population 3,511,532, **rank** 28th

State Symbols
State tree Redbud
State flower Mistletoe
State bird Scissortailed flycatcher

Oregon

Date of Statehood 1859,
   order 33rd
Area in Square Miles 97,052, **rank** 10th
Population 3,559,596, **rank** 27th

State Symbols
State tree Douglas fir
State flower Oregon grape
State bird Western meadowlark

Pennsylvania

Date of Statehood 1787,
   order 2nd
Area in Square Miles 45,308, **rank** 33rd
Population 12,365,455, **rank** 6th

State Symbols
State tree Hemlock
State flower Mountain laurel
State bird Ruffed grouse

Rhode Island

Date of Statehood 1790,
   order 13th
Area in Square Miles 1,213, **rank** 50th
Population 1,076,164, **rank** 43rd

State Symbols
State tree Red maple
State flower Violet
State bird Rhode Island Red

South Carolina

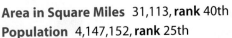

Date of Statehood 1788,
   order 8th
Area in Square Miles 31,113, **rank** 40th
Population 4,147,152, **rank** 25th

State Symbols
State tree Palmetto
State flower Yellow jessamine
State bird Carolina wren

South Dakota

Date of Statehood 1889,
   order 40th
Area in Square Miles 77,122, **rank** 16th
Population 764,309, **rank** 46th

State Symbols
State tree Black Hills spruce
State flower American pasqueflower
State bird Ring-necked pheasant

Tennessee

Date of Statehood 1796,
   order 16th
Area in Square Miles 42,146, **rank** 34th
Population 5,841,748, **rank** 16th

State Symbols
State tree Tulip poplar
State flower Iris
State bird Mockingbird

Texas

Date of Statehood 1845,
   order 28th
Area in Square Miles 266,874, **rank** 2nd
Population 22,118,509, **rank** 2nd

State Symbols

State tree Pecan
State flower Bluebonnet
State bird Mockingbird

Utah

Date of Statehood 1896,
   order 45th
Area in Square Miles 84,905, **rank** 11th
Population 2,351,467, **rank** 34th

State Symbols

State tree Blue spruce
State flower Sego lily
State bird Seagull

Vermont

Date of Statehood 1791,
   order 14th
Area in Square Miles 9,615, **rank** 43rd
Population 619,107, **rank** 49th

State Symbols

State tree Sugar maple
State flower Red clover
State bird Hermit thrush

Virginia

Date of Statehood 1788,
   order 10th
Area in Square Miles 40,598, **rank** 36th
Population 7,386,330, **rank** 12th

State Symbols

State tree Flowering dogwood
State flower Flowering dogwood
State bird Cardinal

Washington

Date of Statehood 1889,
   order 42nd
Area in Square Miles 68,126, **rank** 20th
Population 6,131,445, **rank** 15th

State Symbols

State tree Western hemlock
State flower Coast rhododendron
State bird Willow goldfinch or wild canary

West Virginia

Date of Statehood 1863,
   order 35th
Area in Square Miles 24,231, **rank** 41st
Population 1,810,354, **rank** 37th

State Symbols

State tree Sugar maple
State flower Rhododendron
State bird Cardinal

Wisconsin

Date of Statehood 1848,
   order 30th
Area in Square Miles 56,145, **rank** 26th
Population 5,472,299, **rank** 20th

State Symbols

State tree Sugar maple
State flower Wood violet
State bird Robin

Wyoming

Date of Statehood 1890,
   order 44th
Area in Square Miles 97,914, **rank** 9th
Population 501,242, **rank** 50th

State Symbols

State tree Cottonwood
State flower Indian paintbrush
State bird Western meadowlark

Territories and Possessions of the United States of America

District of Columbia

Status federal district
Area in Square Miles 68
Population 563,384

Symbols
Tree Scarlet oak
Flower American beauty rose
Bird Wood thrush

American Virgin Islands

Status territory
Area in Square Miles 151
Population 124,778

Symbols
Tree n.a.
Flower Yellow elder
Bird Yellow breast

Puerto Rico

Status commonwealth
Area in Square Miles 3,515
Population 3,878,532

Symbols
Tree Ceiba
Flower Maga
Bird Reinita

Guam

Status territory
Area in Square Miles 209
Population 163,941

Symbols
Tree Ifit (Intsiabijuga)
Flower Puti Tai Nobio (Bougainvillea)
Bird Toto (Fruit dove)

Northern Marianas

Status commonwealth
Area in Square Miles 184
Population 78,252

Symbols
Tree n.a.
Flower n.a.
Bird n.a.

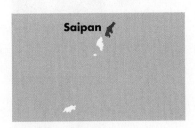

American Samoa

Status territory
Area in Square Miles 77
Population 57,902

Symbols
Tree Ava
Flower Paogo
Bird n.a.

n.a. = not applicable/not available

193

Presidents of the United States

1

George Washington
Years in Office: 1789–1797

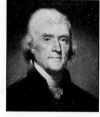

2

John Adams
Years in Office: 1797–1801

3

Thomas Jefferson
Years in Office: 1801–1809

4

James Madison
Years in Office: 1809–1817

5

James Monroe
Years in Office: 1817–1825

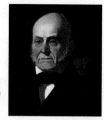

6

John Quincy Adams
Years in Office: 1825–1829

7

Andrew Jackson
Years in Office: 1829–1837

8

Martin Van Buren
Years in Office: 1837–1841

9

William Henry Harrison
Years in Office: 1841

10

John Tyler
Years in Office: 1841–1845

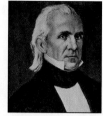

11

James K. Polk
Years in Office: 1845–1849

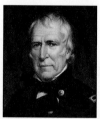

12

Zachary Taylor
Years in Office: 1849–1850

13

Millard Fillmore
Years in Office: 1850–1853

14

Franklin Pierce
Years in Office: 1853–1857

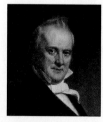

15

James Buchanan
Years in Office: 1857–1861

 **16**

Abraham Lincoln
Years in Office: 1861–1865

 **17**

Andrew Johnson
Years in Office: 1865–1869

 **18**

Ulysses S. Grant
Years in Office: 1869–1877

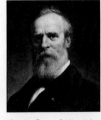 **19**

Rutherford B. Hayes
Years in Office: 1877–1881

 **20**

James A. Garfield
Years in Office: 1881

 **21**

Chester A. Arthur
Years in Office: 1881–1885

 **22**

Grover Cleveland
Years in Office: 1885–1889

 **23**

Benjamin Harrison
Years in Office: 1889–1893

 **24**

Grover Cleveland
Years in Office: 1893–1897

 **25**

William McKinley
Years in Office: 1897–1901

 **26**

Theodore Roosevelt
Years in Office: 1901–1909

 **27**

William Howard Taft
Years in Office: 1909–1913

 **28**

Woodrow Wilson
Years in Office: 1913–1921

 **29**

Warren G. Harding
Years in Office: 1921–1923

 **30**

Calvin Coolidge
Years in Office: 1923–1929

31

Herbert Hoover
Years in Office: 1929–1933

32

Franklin D. Roosevelt
Years in Office: 1933–1945

33

Harry S Truman
Years in Office: 1945–1953

34

Dwight D. Eisenhower
Years in Office: 1953–1961

35

John F. Kennedy
Years in Office: 1961–1963

36

Lyndon B. Johnson
Years in Office: 1963–1969

37

Richard M. Nixon
Years in Office: 1969–1974

38

Gerald R. Ford
Years in Office: 1974–1977

39

Jimmy Carter
Years in Office: 1977–1981

40

Ronald Reagan
Years in Office: 1981–1989

41

George Bush
Years in Office: 1989–1993

42

William J. Clinton
Years in Office: 1993–2001

43

George W. Bush
Years in Office: 2001–

abolitionists page 103
Abolitionists were people who worked to end slavery in the United States.

amendments page 68
Amendments are laws that are added to the Constitution.

American Revolution page 43
The American Revolution was the war that the American colonies fought against Great Britain from 1775 to 1781.

assured page 50
Assured means made sure or certain.

battlefields page 140
Battlefields are areas of land on which battles are fought.

Bill of Rights page 68
The Bill of Rights is the first ten amendments added to the Constitution.

body of water page 32
A body of water is a large area of water. Lakes, rivers, and oceans are bodies of water.

border page 93
A border is a line that separates one state from another. A border can also separate cities, towns, and countries.

Boston Tea Party page 42
During the Boston Tea Party, Americans went on three British tea ships. They threw all the tea into the ocean because they did not want to pay a tea tax.

boundaries page 61
Boundaries are the lines around a city, state, or country. Rivers, oceans, and mountains can be boundaries. Boundaries are often shown as lines drawn on maps.

branches of government page 67
The three branches of government in the United States are Congress, the President, and the Supreme Court, as well as the people who work for them.

buffalo page 5
Buffalo are oxen. They are large animals with horns and fur.

canals page 90
Canals are waterways that connect bodies of water, such as rivers.

capital page 17
The capital of a country or a state is the city where the government meets.

captured page 80
Captured means took and held a person, place, or thing by using force.

Church of England page 20
The Church of England is all the churches in England that accept the ruler of England as the head of the church.

citizens page 118
Citizens are members of a country.

Civil War page 139
The Civil War was the war fought between the North and the South from 1861 to 1865.

claimed page 11
When a country claimed land, it meant it would own and rule that land.

climate page 134
Climate is the usual weather in an area.

coast page 123
A coast is land along an ocean.

colony page 21
A colony is land ruled by another nation.

commander in chief page 59
The commander in chief is the most important leader of the American army.

Congress page 66
Congress is the United States Senate and House of Representatives. Men and women in Congress write laws for the United States.

Constitution page 55
A constitution is a set of laws. The United States Constitution is a set of laws for the United States.

Constitutional Convention page 60
The Constitutional Convention was a set of important meetings in 1787. During the meetings, American leaders wrote a set of new laws for the United States.

cotton page 5
Cotton is a plant used to make cloth. You can wear clothes made of cotton.

cotton gin page 88
A cotton gin is a machine that removes seeds from cotton plants.

crops page 75
Crops are plants grown by farmers. Corn, potatoes, and cotton are three kinds of crops.

dams page 126
Dams are strong walls built to hold back water in rivers.

Declaration of Independence page 46
The Declaration of Independence was an important paper that said the American colonies were a free nation.

departure page 81
Departure means leaving.

destroyed page 140
Destroyed means ruined. A war can destroy homes, farms, and cities.

doubled page 76
When the United States doubled in size, it became twice as large as it had been.

education page 102
Education is the learning a person gets from school, people, and places.

electric sparks page 54
Electric sparks are tiny bits of electricity that give off small amounts of light for a few seconds.

Emancipation Proclamation page 140
The Emancipation Proclamation was a paper that said all slaves in the Confederate States were free. It went into effect in 1863.

environment page 126
The environment is the land, water, and climate of an area.

equal page 46
People who are equal have the same importance.

escape page 132
To escape means to get free.

First Lady page 61
The wife of the President of the United States is called the First Lady.

fort page 112
A fort is a building from which an army can fight its enemies.

freedom of religion page 20
Freedom of religion means one can pray the way he or she wants to pray.

freedom of the press page 68
Freedom of the press means a person can write what he or she wants to write in newspapers and books.

freedom of the seas page 80
Freedom of the seas means that people can sail ships wherever they want.

Fugitive Slave Act page 132
The Fugitive Slave Act was a law passed in 1850. It said that all escaped slaves must be returned to the South.

Gadsden Purchase page 118
The Gadsden Purchase was land that the United States bought from Mexico.

general page 47
A general is an important army leader.

geographers page 17
Geographers are people who study different areas and people on Earth.

goal page 140
A goal is something a person wants and tries to get.

gold rush page 125
A gold rush is a time when many people move into an area in order to find gold.

goods page 87
Goods are things people buy.

governor page 21
A governor is a government leader for a state, town, or area.

Great Spirit page 84
Many Native Americans believe in the Great Spirit, their most important god. They believe the Great Spirit made them and placed them on the land.

hasten page 81
To hasten means to hurry.

House of Representatives page 66
The House of Representatives is one of the two houses, or parts, of Congress. It has 435 members.

human/environment interaction page 126
The geography theme of human/environment interaction tells how people can change an area. It also tells how people live in an area.

in debt page 27
A person who is in debt owes money to other people.

independent page 46
Independent means free. An independent country rules itself.

Industrial Revolution page 87
The Industrial Revolution was a change from making goods by hand to making goods by machine.

insist page 81
To insist means to demand.

invented page 87
Invented means thought up or made for the first time.

justices page 67
Justices are judges. There are nine justices in the Supreme Court.

lame page 50
Lame means hurt. If a person's feet or legs are lame, it is hard for that person to walk.

location page 62
The geography theme of location tells where a place is found.

locomotives page 90
Locomotives are engines used to pull trains.

Louisiana Purchase page 76
The Louisiana Purchase was the sale of a large piece of land west of the Mississippi River. The United States bought it from France in 1803.

Loyalists page 47
Loyalists were Americans who did not want the 13 colonies to become independent. Loyalists helped Great Britain during the American Revolution.

manage page 58
To manage means to control and take care of something.

Manifest Destiny page 116
Manifest Destiny was the idea that the United States should rule land from the Atlantic Ocean to the Pacific Ocean.

mass production page 88
In mass production, people or machines make many goods that are exactly alike.

Mayflower Compact page 21
The Mayflower Compact was the Pilgrims' plan for ruling themselves in America.

mental illness page 103
People with mental illness have a disease or condition that changes the way they think.

Mexican Cession page 118
The Mexican Cession was land that the United States got as a result of the Mexican War.

miners page 126
Miners are people who dig in the earth to find gold or other metals or stones.

miserable page 84
To be miserable is to be unhappy.

missions page 16
Missions are places where people teach others how to become Christians.

movement page 97
The geography theme of movement tells how people, goods, and ideas move from one place to another.

nation page 40
A nation is a large group of people living together in one country.

navy page 81
The navy is a nation's warships and all the people who work on the warships.

New World page 11
People in Europe called North America and South America the New World because they had not known about these continents.

Oregon Trail page 122
The Oregon Trail was the trail that wagons followed through the West to Oregon.

oxen page 122
An ox is an animal like a cow. Oxen is the word used for more than one ox.

Parliament page 41
The people who write laws for Great Britain are called Parliament. They work in the Parliament Building.

pass page 125
A pass is a trail through mountains.

peace treaty page 22
A peace treaty is an agreement not to fight.

peril page 114
To peril means to put in danger.

place page 17
The geography theme of place tells what makes an area different from other areas in the world.

plantations page 130
Plantations are very large farms where crops such as cotton and sugar cane are grown.

port page 42
A port is a place by an ocean or river where ships are loaded and unloaded.

priests page 16
Priests are people who lead religious services and teach about the Catholic religion.

primary sources page 28
Primary sources are the words and objects of people who have lived at different times. Some primary sources are journals, letters, and tools.

printer page 53
A printer is a person who prints books and newspapers.

printing shop page 53
A printing shop is a place with machines for printing books and newspapers.

promptly page 114
Promptly means soon.

property page 119
All the land and other things a person owns are his or her property.

provisions page 114
Provisions are food and other supplies.

published page 53
Published means prepared a book or newspaper so it could be sold.

quarreling page 130
Quarreling means arguing or not agreeing about something.

race page 84
A race is a group of people sharing the same beginnings from long ago. They usually have similar eyes and skin color.

rebuild page 141
To rebuild means to build something again.

recovered page 50
Recovered means got better.

reform page 101
Reform is a change to make something, such as a school or government, better.

region page 134
The geography theme of region tells how places in an area are alike.

relief page 114
Relief is help from others.

religions page 4
Religions are the ways people believe in and pray to a god or to many gods.

religious page 26
Religious means having to do with religion.

representatives page 66
People who make laws in the House of Representatives are called representatives.

republic page 113
A republic is a country where people vote for their leaders. These leaders make laws for the people and lead the government.

secured page 81
Something that has been secured has been made safe.

Senate page 66
The Senate is one of the two houses, or parts, of Congress. It has 100 members.

senators page 66
People who make laws in the Senate are senators.

settlers page 25
Settlers are people who go to live in a new place.

shortcut page 31
A shortcut is a shorter way to go to a place.

slavery page 16
Slavery is the owning of people, or slaves. Slaves are forced to work without pay.

snowshoes page 33
Snowshoes are wooden frames that a person can attach to shoes to help him or her walk on deep snow.

spices page 9
Spices are added to food to improve the way it tastes and smells.

Stamp Act page 41
The Stamp Act said that Americans in the British colonies had to pay a tax on things made from paper.

steamboat page 89
A steamboat is a boat that is powered by a steam engine.

steam engine page 89
A steam engine is a machine that uses steam to create power for other machines.

sugar cane page 130
People get sugar from the tall plant called sugar cane.

Supreme Court page 67
The Supreme Court is the highest court in the United States. It decides whether laws agree with the Constitution.

surrendered page 59
An army that surrendered in a war stopped fighting and agreed that it lost.

tariffs page 96
Tariffs are taxes on goods from other countries.

tax page 41
Tax is money that a person must pay to the government.

Texas Revolution page 113
The Texas Revolution was the war that Texans fought in order to win their independence from Mexico.

themes page 17
Themes are main ideas. The five themes of geography help geographers learn about areas and people on Earth.

tobacco page 26
Tobacco is a plant. The leaves of this plant are smoked in pipes, cigars, and cigarettes.

Trail of Tears page 96
When the Cherokee were forced to move west to Indian Territory, they called their trip the Trail of Tears.

troops page 50
Troops are soldiers in an army.

Union page 133
The Union is the United States.

unite page 84
To unite is to join together.

victory page 114
A victory is a win.

wagon train page 122
Covered wagons that traveled together on a trail formed a wagon train.

Index

New York City, New York, 59, 61, 90

Niña, 10

North, 103, 130, 131, 132, 133, 134, 135, 138, 139, 140, 141

North America, 34

North Carolina, 93

Northwest, 5, 125

O

Oberlin College, 102

Oglethorpe, James, 27

Ohio, 102

Oklahoma, 95, 98

Oregon, 122–124, 125

Oregon Country, 122–124

Oregon Trail, 122–123, 124, 125

Osceola, 96

P

Pacific Ocean, 77, 116, 118, 119

Parliament, 41, 42, 46, 55, 65, 66

Peace treaty, 22, 49, 60, 83, 118

Penn, William, 27

Pennsylvania, 27, 47, 50, 54, 59

Philadelphia, Pennsylvania, 47, 54, 55, 60, 65

Pilgrims, 20–22, 25

Pinta, 10

Pitcher, Molly, 48

Plantations, 130–131, 134, 140

Plymouth, Massachusetts, 21, 22

Poland, 48, 49

Polk, James K., 117, 118, 124

Potomac River, 62

President, Constitution and the, 67

Prison reform, 103

Providence, Rhode Island, 26

Pueblo Indians, 17

Puritans, 26

Q

Quakers, 27

R

Railroads, 90, 118, 119, 134, 139

Reform, 101–104

Representatives, 66

Republic of Texas, 113, 116

Rhode Island, 26

Richmond, Virginia, 140

Rio Grande, 117, 118

Rocky Mountains, 77, 122

S

Sacagawea, 77

St. Lawrence River, 31, 32

St. Louis, Missouri, 32, 34

Salomon, Haym, 49

Sampson, Deborah, 48

Sangre de Cristo Mountains, 17

San Jacinto River, 113

San Miguel Mission, 17

Santa Anna, Antonio López de, 112, 113, 114, 116

Santa Fe, 16, 17

Santa María, 10

Schools, 26, 54, 101–103, 132
    for girls, 102

Seminole, 96

Senate, 66

Senators, 66

Seneca Falls, New York, 104

Sequoyah, 94–95

Serra, Father Junipero, 16

Shawnee, 84

Shoshone, 77

Slater, Samuel, 88

Slave(s), 16, 26, 33, 76, 83, 103, 111, 130–132, 134, 135, 140

Slavery, 16, 61, 101, 103, 130–133, 135, 139, 140
South, 93, 103, 130, 131, 132, 133, 134–135, 138, 139, 140, 141
South America, 14
South Carolina, 93, 96, 138
Southeast, 15, 95, 96, 97
Southwest, 5, 14, 15, 16, 17, 118, 119
Spain, 10, 11, 14, 15, 16, 34, 75, 94, 110
Spanish, 14, 15–16, 17, 31, 33, 48
    language, 111
Squanto, 22
Stamp Act, 41, 55
Standing Bear, Luther, 6
Stanton, Elizabeth Cady, 104
"Star-Spangled Banner, The," 83
Steamboat, 89
Steam engine, 89, 90
Steuben, Friedrich von, 48
Supreme Court, United States, 67
Sutter Creek, California, 127

T

Tahlequah, Oklahoma, 98
Tariffs, 96
Taxes, 41, 42, 55, 96
Tea tax, 42
Tecumseh, 81–84
Texan(s), 111, 112, 113, 114, 116
Texas, 16, 110–113, 116, 117, 118
Texas Declaration of Independence, 112, 113, 114
Texas Revolution, 112–113
Thanksgiving, 22
Trail of Tears, 96, 97–98
Travis, William Barrett, 114

Trenton, New Jersey, 59
Tubman, Harriet, 132

U

Union, 133, 138–141
Utah, 118

V

Valley Forge, Pennsylvania, 50
Virginia, 25, 34, 58, 59, 60, 61, 62, 63, 139, 141
Voting rights
    for women, 104

W

Waldo, Albigence, 50
Wampanoag, 22
War of 1812, 80–83, 93
Washington, 124
Washington, D.C., 61, 62–63, 67, 82
Washington, George, 34, 47, 50, 58–61, 62, 63, 82
Washington, Martha, 59, 60, 61
West, 74, 77, 96, 125, 131, 133
White House, 67, 82
Whitman, Narcissa, 123
Whitney, Eli, 88–89
Willard, Emma, 102
Williams, Roger, 26
Women's rights, 101, 104, 119

Y

York, 77
Yorktown, Virginia, 60